High Frequency Words

Strategies that build skills in spelling, vocabulary, and word play

Ken Marland

Pembroke Publishers Limited

© 2002 Pembroke Publishers
538 Hood Road
Markham, Ontario, Canada L3R 3K9
www.pembrokepublishers.com

Distributed in the U.S. by Stenhouse Publishers
477 Congress Street
Portland, ME 04101
www.stenhouse.com

We acknowledge the financial support of the Government of Canada through the Book Publishing Industry Development Program (BPIDP) for our publishing activities.

National Library of Canada Cataloguing in Publication

Marland, Ken, 1952–
   High frequency words : strategies that build skills in spelling, vocabulary and word play / Ken Marland.

ISBN 1-55138-144-3

1. Vocabulary – Study and teaching (Elementary)   2. English Language – Word frequency.
I. Title.

LB1576.M348 2002   372.44   C2002-902897-3

Editor: Cynthia Young
Cover Design: John Zehethofer
Typesetting: Jay Tee Graphics

Printed and bound in Canada
9 8 7 6 5 4 3 2 1

Table of Contents

Part Three — Student Activity Sheets

Part Four — Teacher Evaluation Tools

Table of Contents

Part Three — Student Activity Sheets

Part Four — Teacher Evaluation Tools

Learning to Spell

The Power of Spelling

Good spellers use a variety of mental strategies to remember how to spell words. They use their spelling skills as a bridge that links their oral vocabulary to their written work. An extensive oral vocabulary facilitates good oral expression, and good spelling skills facilitate clear written expression. Conversely, the student who is unable to apply spelling skills can be limited in his or her academic achievement. A child who uses "awesome" orally, might not use that word in written work — especially if he or she has received negative feedback for misspelled words. The child is likely to choose a word such as "nice" because it is easier to spell.

Weak spellers view spelling as arbitrary, haphazard, difficult, unlearnable, and beyond their control. Good spellers have internalized a set of cognitive tools that helps them to visualize words, use an analogy, break up the words, and/or understand the words in context.

Whether the words relate to social studies or mathematics (or any other subject), understanding how to use spelling skills enhances a student's overall learning and development. When students understand, recognize, and make use of correct spellings, they are problem solving, using their brains to decipher and connect visual and auditory cues, conceptual understanding, and human expression. Students will carry solid spelling skills from subject to subject and grade to grade, and these skills will facilitate the student's lifelong learning process.

> Rather than teach students to spell specific words, it is more effective to teach them that **they can learn** to spell.

The Brain and Learning to Spell

Spelling, unlike breathing, is not the result of an inherent brain function. We are not born knowing how to read, write, or spell. Before humans developed literacy and numeracy, they had to organize and categorize incoming information to make it useful or meaningful. This information processing is a cognitive activity.

The brain functions that are used for processing memory and emotions play an important role in learning. The brain stores memory in many ways, and several factors enhance or detract from our capacity for memory. A relaxed and safe environment can do much to improve students' learning. Similarly, humor and novelty may stimulate interest and improve memory. Distractions (ranging from hunger to noise from classmates) can be enough to disrupt a student's memory-making thinking.

> Reading, mathematics, and spelling are not *brain functions*, but are instead *cognitive activities* generated by various brain functions.
>
> The brain is the organ that *learns* to spell.

Multiple Intelligences and Learning Styles

Howard Gardner suggests that there are a variety of intelligences, including verbal-linguistic, mathematical, visual-spatial, bodily-kinesthetic, musical, interpersonal, and intrapersonal. These innate intelligences cause both teachers and students to approach new information and learning in a variety of ways. The following table identifies the different intelligences and the kinds of learning activities associated with the specific intelligences.

Verbal-Linguistic	Mathematical	Visual-Spatial	Bodily-Kinesthetic	Musical	Interpersonal	Intrapersonal
• listening • linguistic humor • storytelling	• problem solving • patterns • graphic organizers	• visualization • imagination • visual illustrations	• hands on • actions and/or illustrations • using body	• illustrating with sound • rhythm • rhyme	• group work • discussion • cooperative learning	• metacognition • tasks of concentration • self-identification reporting

How the brain learns and remembers information, such as the spelling of a word, is a complex process. Gardner's theory of multiple intelligences gives us a sense of both the complexity of learning as well as how we can facilitate learning by using a variety of strategies that appeal to the different ways that students learn. Although some individuals excel in certain of these intelligences, along with the majority of people they acquire skills and knowledge through the use of all the intelligences. This is why it is important to present material in a variety of ways — not because there may be a certain genius in the class, but because such an approach is the most brain-friendly method, and it maximizes the ways in which students learn and remember information.

The following table indicates how several of the intelligences can be incorporated in teaching one word, "**yellow.**"

Intelligence	How It Can Be Used

Verbal-Linguistic	• phonics; associate sounds with letters
	
	• oral discussion about the word and use of verbal descriptions
	
	• humor — *Teacher*: What is the first letter in the word "yellow"?
	    Student: **Y** [why?].
	    Teacher: Because I want to know what the first letter is.

Mathematics	• six letters; three "pairs" **ye + ll + ow** • first pair is an odd pair with two different letters (**ye**); letters in the second pair are the same (**ll**); third pair is an odd pair with two different letters (**ow**) • symmetry of the word: number of letters is divisible by two (**yel + low**)
Visual-Spatial	• use the image of a teeter-totter • "ll" is the plank • the plank must be balanced on each side…two letters on either side of the ll • common error (**yello**) can be corrected with the concept of balancing the teeter totter (**ye + ll + ow**)
Bodily-Kinesthetic	• use the concept of a balanced teeter-totter • assign students to role-play a letter from the word yellow • students arrange themselves to spell the word correctly • "unbalance" the word by leaving out a letter; then balance the word by asking all the letters to stand up in their correct positions

Intelligence	How It Can Be Used

Musical	• discuss the up and down motion of a teeter-totter
	
	• the two syllables in yellow are up and down — the emphasis is on the first syllable, and the second syllable drops as we say
	
	    yel
	       low
	
	• students can clap the rhythm of the word and compare it to other words as they say phrases "yellow yellow little fellow" versus "blue blue old man."

Interpersonal*	• working in groups (as in role-playing the letters) • sharing and hearing ideas during discussion • offering suggestions for strategies, letter or word associations, etc.
Intrapersonal*	• individual student considers ways that help him/her to remember how to spell the word • choosing the method that works best for the individual person • recognizing that other students may use a different method because each person has a unique way to learn and remember spelling patterns

* Note that both the interpersonal and intrapersonal intelligences form the basis for all the spelling lessons described in this book. Each lesson includes discussion and group work, and, ultimately, an individual selection of a spelling strategy.

Metacognition

Give a student a mathematical problem to solve and, when she has arrived at an answer, ask her *how* she solved the problem. Her mathematical answer is the result of her mental activity. Her explanation of *how* she solved the problem is metacognition. Metacognition is the term used to describe "the process of thinking about one's thinking."

Students who can articulate the processes or strategies they use to spell certain words are demonstrating "spelling metacognition." A student might remember how to spell **again** by associating it with **rain**. Some students might do this through the rhyme alone. Others might add a mental picture of a cloud and the question, "Will it **rain again**?"

Many students, especially those with weak spelling skills, view spelling as a random act that is based on rote memorization and chance. Metacognition can help these students implement a variety of strategies for remembering how to spell different words. Students can use metacognition to match the spelling of a word to a memory-aid that fits their learning style preferences.

Mediated Learning and Cognitive Development

Children learn in almost any situation. What they learn and how well they learn is affected by several factors, such as their preferred learning styles, personal interests, "intelligences," age and development…and the teaching and learning situation itself. Rueven Feuerstein believes that a child's intellectual development depends on interaction between the child and an adult. This interaction, known as mediated learning, is supported by a strong body of research. According to Feuerstein, when a child learns directly from the environment, with no outside help, it is *direct learning.* Note that this is different from *direct instruction,* in which a teacher specifically tells a specific group of students how to do something. In spelling, direct instruction would mean assigning students the task of unscrambling the words on a worksheet to find the correct spellings. For students who know how to spell the words, this is a practice activity. However, students who do not know the correct spellings must try to learn directly from the activity. As the task becomes frustrating, these students feel badly about themselves because they cannot complete the worksheet.

Such direct instruction does not provide students with the opportunity to interact with their environment. "Direct learning" frequently occurs through trial and error, observation, and conditioning as the student interacts alone with the environment. It can be a frustrating experience for the child. Students who learn only from direct experience demonstrate a passive learning style and do not become actively involved or take responsibility for their learning.

In mediated learning situations, intentional and deliberate activity occurs between a nurturing adult and a child, and it leads to the development of many cognitive skills that form the foundation of intellectual development. An adult could send a child alone to the corner store to buy a package of muffins. But consider how things change when an adult makes muffins with the child. It is easy to see that making muffins with the child has the greater potential for enhancing the child's cognitive development.

Making muffins with the adult gives the child many experiences. In addition, the adult is present to highlight and point out certain features, as well as to teach skills that could be applied in new situations. The adult might talk about the egg and its shell, thus encouraging the child to develop and use observation skills. The child might learn about long-term goals because he must delay gratification until the muffins are cooked and cooled. Numeracy skills are inherent in measuring the ingredients. Telling and measuring time while the muffins cook can also be introduced.

Social interaction skills are also part of the muffin-making experience. In mediated learning, children interact with the teacher to learn new strategies that can be applied in other situations. The students find the experience has a greater sense of meaning because they are involved in the discussion and the task. During the muffin-making experience, the child may learn the names of cooking utensils, practice good manners (please and thank you) or how to eat, and so on.

Children's vocabulary also tends to grow in mediated learning situations. Their oral vocabulary is developed through oral interactions with the adult. For example, a child who wanders through a museum by herself will not develop the same understanding and vocabulary as a child who is accompanied by an adult who intentionally discusses the displays and makes them relevant to that child's experience. Through such mediated learning interactions, the child develops an expressive oral vocabulary from which to select words for use in a written story.

The interaction between the teacher and the children in the lessons in this book creates a mediated learning experience in which the students and the teacher interact on an equal footing. There is direct *instruction*

It takes about 60 repetitions for an athlete to remember a specific muscle movement. Children need up to 40 opportunities to write a word with its correct spelling before they can remember it.

(introduction of words, prelude to discussion, closing the lesson), but the lesson evolves from the active participation of the students in sharing their ideas and discussing strategies. This mediated learning environment is intended to generate strategies that the children can use to remember the correct spelling of a specific word and then apply to new words in the future.

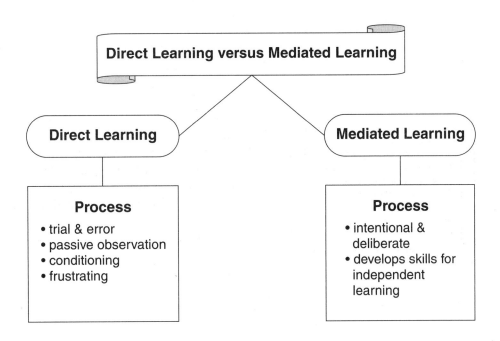

Learning to Spell—Rules and Tools

Caught Versus Taught?

How much of spelling is caught versus taught? A child is explicitly taught about 3800 words in twelve years of school. The average adult uses between 10 000 and 20 000 words. Therefore, much spelling competency must be self-taught through a problem-solving behavior. However, in the early stages of learning to spell, children must be taught the skills that will enable them to spell new words in later grades, when there is no longer a word list, but rather an assumption that the children already know how to spell high frequency words and can generate the correct spellings of new words.

A Word About Spelling Rules

Spelling "rules" are one type of tool among the many that teachers can offer students. In general, these "rules" work — except for the "*exceptions* to the rule." This can be a problem for some young children, who usually consider "rules" as set, fixed, and unbreakable. Primary-grade students are very rule-conscious as is often indicated by the frequent tattle-tales a classroom teacher hears. It may be difficult for some primary students to understand that sometimes the rules are broken when we spell some words.

> It is important for teachers (and students) to recognize that *no single strategy* will teach students how to spell *all* words, especially in the English language. Teachers put students at a disadvantage if they do not teach a variety of spelling strategies.

To avoid confusion, it is perhaps better to call the "rules" *probabilities*. Thus, you might say that when we hear an **r** sound at the end of a word, "It is *probably spelled* with an **–er** ending. When the same **r** sound is in the middle of the word, "It is *probably spelled* with **–ir** *or* **–ur**." Students who learn and understand the idea of "spelling probabilities" rather than "spelling rules" are less rigid in their thinking and are better able to use a variety of strategies in learning to spell.

The Power to Learn — Tools for Spelling

To learn to spell, students need three sets of tools: cognitive tools, technological tools, and organizational tools.

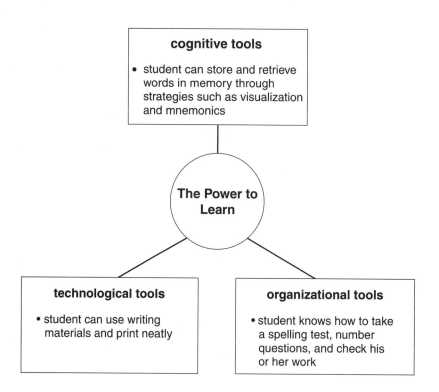

Cognitive Tools The cognitive tools include memory and thinking strategies (visualization, attention, perseverance). Cognitive tools may also include "self-talk" or talking to oneself mentally.

Technological Tools Technological tools include equipment (pencils, paper, chalkboards, chalk). But, the most important technological tool is printing by hand. There are two reasons why students need to print precisely: i) clear printing of the correct spelling of the word provides the brain with a strong visual image, and ii) printing generates a stronger tactile and kinesthetic signal for the brain. Students who form their letters correctly also tend to be the better spellers. This may be a result of the increased concentration required to form the letters carefully, which in turn encourages greater focus on the task at hand: the correct spelling of the word. Weak spellers tend to have weak

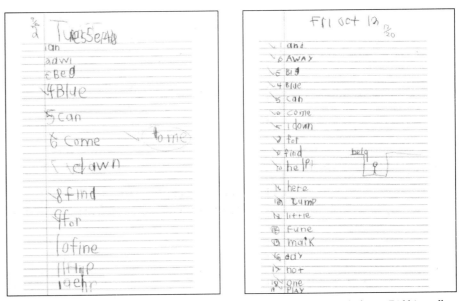

This student's spelling and printing improved dramatically over a short period of time. Did his spelling improve because his letter formations provided a clearer and more precise image for his brain?

printing skills. The figure above shows two samples from the same student. Note how the student's spelling improved dramatically as did his printing. Students need to be taught to use their technological tools effectively.

Organizational Tools   Organizational tools refer to skills needed for taking a spelling test; preparing materials for the accurate and efficient completion of assignments; completing a task by following steps in sequence; and maintaining order with the materials to be used.

These skills must be taught — especially in the primary grades. Students who have weak organizational skills tend to miss much of the teaching and, therefore, the learning. While these students are looking for their pencils, the teacher may be explaining a new strategy for remembering the spelling of a word. Rather than skipping a word that is causing difficulties on a test, some students "freeze" on the unknown word and fall behind for all the following words, thus minimizing their overall success.

Teaching Strategies for Spelling

Using Metacognition

An important part of spelling instruction is teaching students how metacognition — in this context, thinking about strategies for learning — can improve their spelling skills. When a student can describe a spelling strategy or process, she knows it well enough to apply it to learning a new word. These strategies can be taught, and students can learn how to use them in ways that support their own learning needs. The lessons in this book are designed to facilitate the instruction of the strategies, as well as to help students learn how to use metacognition in their spelling lessons.

Each strategy that students use actually ensures that they spend time thinking about how they will remember the spelling of a given word. Students will hear, print, read, and say the word. They will discuss the word and ways to remember how to spell it. There are several strategies that they can use to remember the correct spelling of a word. The following strategies are used in the lessons in this book.

Phonics Skills

Phonics skills are just one of *several* strategies that children can use in learning to read and spell. There is no single strategy that works for every student and every word. Phonics skills are useful for about 46% of English words, which means that the other 54% of the words require alternative strategies. As well, weak spellers appear to take a different developmental path than average spellers. Phonemic awareness changes little after Grade 5, but visual accuracy scores increase dramatically. Weak spellers continue to increase in phonemic awareness after Grade 5, but their visual accuracy scores remain the same as they were in lower grades.

Visualization

Visualization is seeing something in full with the mind's eye. For example, a movie director creates a scene by "seeing" (imagining) the whole scene and then arranging the set and directing the actors accordingly. When a person remembers how to spell a word by seeing it printed on a screen or page in their mind, that person is using visualization.

Good spellers almost always mention how they visualize words and how they can tell by looking at a word whether it is spelled correctly. Some people are able to visualize going into a restaurant, opening the menu, and seeing the phrase "Today's Special." They can then write down the spelling of **special** by copying it from the menu they visualize. The ability to visualize words seems especially strong in students who are visual learners.

To help students develop this skill in class, have the students correctly spell a word on their chalkboard, erase the word, and then imagine that the word is still on the board. Ask them to imagine themselves writing the word correctly, as they did just a few moments earlier. Encourage them to visualize the word. Can they see the letters in their mind and copy them down?

Good visualization skills and instruction in the spelling of high frequency words lead to increased recognition of those words in reading. It has been demonstrated that students recalled at sight, with greater accuracy, those high frequency words that they were taught to spell compared to those words they were not taught to spell.

Configuration

The shape or configuration of a word is also a useful strategy for some students. It is related to visualization in that the overall shape of the word is sometimes what makes the spelling "look right" (or wrong) to students. Enhancing the ability to remember and recognize the correct configuration of a word is another important reason for students to print neatly and carefully during spelling practice. When neatly printed, the word **can** has a shape that is more like an actual tin can than does **kan**. Similarly, the short-tall-short letters in the word **who** may help students to remember the letter **h** in the word.

Visual Cues

Sometimes students can associate the letters in a word with the meaning, and this may help them recall the correct spelling. Many students use visual cues such as making the "**oo**" in **look** into eyes or a pair of eyeglasses. Some students associate the circles in the letters of **good** with "four cookies." Then they associate the cookies with the meaning of **good**.

Foundation Words

Some words are foundation words that can be used for learning new words. For example, a group of students that masters the spelling of **and** can use **and** later to help them spell **hand**.

Students write the foundation word, and then add one letter to spell **hand**, then **land**, and so on.

Chunking, Patterns, and Word Families

When students have learned a number of foundation words, they can also begin to use chunking, word and letter patterns, and word families as strategies for spelling. Chunking or breaking a word into smaller segments can mean breaking it down into smaller "words within the word," or simply into smaller bits that go together like interlocking building blocks.

A a B b C c D d E e F f G g H h I i J j K k L l M m N n

ear

add one letter and spell **hear**

you **hear** with your **ear**

add one letter and spell **heart**

the doctor can **hear** your **heart**

move the "h" to the end **earth**

This strategy can be of great help to students who have trouble seeing the patterns and relationships between words and word families. It is also useful for learning to spell words that are seemingly unrelated, such as **ear** and **earth**.

Spelling Words by Analogy

Comparing the spelling, sound, shape, letters, number of letters, and patterns can help students understand and remember those aspects of a new word. This kind of word analogy was demonstrated in a class where the students were learning to spell **come**. Some students noticed the word **me** in the word. This led to the phrase **come to me**. When the group looked at **to me**, they realized that if they changed one letter, they would have the word **come**. To remind themselves, they came up with, "I'm teaching my dog to **come to me**."

Modelling and Monitoring

As much as possible, use the spelling words in everyday contexts to model the correctly spelled words for the students. Words studied out of context have minimal effect in helping students develop spelling proficiency. It also is important to check the students' work any time where they may have used a given spelling word.

The example of student work on page 17 shows why it can be more effective and positive to supervise a student one-on-one as opposed to letting the student simply write out the words five or ten times without supervision.

This student did not learn to spell these words correctly. Unsupervised, he practiced spelling some words incorrectly. He also developed a negative attitude toward spelling because of the tedious nature of the task and his lack of success at it.

Contextual Clues

With some words, the context is not crucial if the child hears the word clearly, as in **"Said. He *said* he would go with me. Said."** For true homonyms, and words that sound similar, context is very important, as in **wear**, **where**, and **were**.

Unfortunately, many students listen for the word, but ignore the context in which the word is used. Students with weak spelling skills will often overlook the context and impulsively spell the word they think they heard. Teach students to question the context when you ask them to spell a homonym such as **here** versus **hear**. Pause after saying the word, but do not give the contextual sentence. Wait for the students to ask, "Which one?" before you provide a contextual clue, such as "I left my boots **here** by the door," or "I **hear** a noise at the door." This technique encourages students to be aware of homonyms and to be attentive to the sentence that provides context for the spelling word.

Mathematics, Numbers, and Patterns

The use of numbers and patterns can help some students remember the correct spelling of some words. The word **four** has four letters, which distinguishes it from the word **for**. (See page 8 for using mathematics as a strategy to teach the word **yellow**.)

Kinesthetics

Body movements can provide two strategies for helping students remember how to spell a word. The first strategy focuses on the movements and positions of the mouth (tongue, teeth, lips, and jaw) as we speak. Teaching children to become aware of these movements and positions as they say a word can help many students, especially those who may have difficulty hearing some sounds. Students sometimes have difficulty hearing the **l** sound, especially when it is attached to another consonant, as in the word **blue**. Pronounce the word carefully, and ask students to repeat it. They should notice the position of the tongue, which is touching the back of the front teeth just before the vowel sound. When the student feels the tongue in that position, he or she knows there is an **l** in the word.

Body movement may also include large motions that help to illustrate a word. For example, kinesthetics can help students remember that **day** ends with **y**. Have students role play getting out of bed with a big stretch, with their arms overhead so they look like the letter **Y**. As the students stretch, ask them to remember, "We start each **day** with a big stretch."

Music, Rhyme, and Rhythm

Music, rhyme, and rhythm are closely related to word families. If students are musically oriented they can develop a series of words that have a rhyming or rhythm pattern, or can count and clap syllables in words. (See page 9 for an example of the use of music to teach the word **yellow**.) It is often helpful to use simple or familiar poems to develop a sense of rhyme, such as Little Boy Blue come blow your horn, the cows in the meadow are eating the _____?

Storytelling

Children (and many adults) find it easier to remember stories than isolated bits of information. In spelling, many children find it helpful if the teacher (or they themselves) create a story that gives clues about the spelling of a word. Key details of the story (and sometimes the sequence) help students to remember the letters that spell a particular word. One example is the story suggested in the lesson for **help**. In the story, a man (**he**) helps a boy who has fallen down a steep cliff. The man needs a rope (**l**), which he unwinds (**p**) and uses to pull the boy up. In the lesson for **any**, the foundation word **ant** is a key detail in the story. The last letter is changed to **y** to make **any**, and the children can associate this with **Yip**, the name of the main character. This strategy can be used for almost any word, as long as the story itself is memorable to the children because of humor, novelty, or silliness. Ideally, the story uses the spelling word in a logical (even if imaginative) context.

Mnemonics

A mnemonic is a device or tool — often a phrase — that helps a person remember specific information. The phrase gives meaning to, or identifies a pattern in, otherwise confusing material. Mnemonic phrases are often used by good spellers for tricky words. One phrase that works well for remembering the "**ie**" in *believe* is "You would never **bel*ie*ve** a **lie**.

Mnemonics are often the last step in a *series* of strategies (e.g., mathematics —> chunking —> mnemonic) for remembering the correct spelling. Students may recall the "**e**" at the end of **one** more easily if they know that there are *three* letters, if they chunk the word as **on + e**, and use a mnemonic; for example, "When you play hopscotch, you start *on on*e."

Additional Strategies for Spelling Instruction

Tactile Awareness
Our faces and tongue move in certain ways to make sounds. Children can use this information when they learn to spell. This works with any word. For example, when you say the word **they** your tongue is pressed between your upper and lower front teeth.

Etymology
The history behind the development of a given word can be fascinating. Studying the evolution of a word can be helpful, especially when the spelling is not typical according to its phonics or the "rules." For example, **white** developed from a Celtic word that meant "shining bright." However, it was pronounced **h-wite**, with a gutteral **h**. Over time, the h-sound was lost in the oral language, and the spelling became **white**, as we know it today.

Pronunciation
Tactile awareness, noted above, does not always reflect the correct sound-letter association. The pronunciation of a word can be affected by a speaker's regional dialect, a foreign accent, or even speech problems. Consider the words **jumped** and **butter. Jumped** sounds as though it should have a **t** at the end. When some people say **butter**, it sounds like **budder**. Students need to know that some words are not spelled the way they are spoken.

Words in Context of a Subject Area
Whenever possible, point out the spelling of key words in a subject area. In science, **hibernate** could be replaced by **sleep all winter**. By providing strategies for spelling **hibernate** in science, students are more able and encouraged to use and spell more technical language. In social studies, sometimes history has a role in determining the name of a place. St. John's, Newfoundland, was founded on the feast day of St. John the Baptist — St. John's Day. That is why it is spelled in the possessive form with the apostrophe.

Coaching
Think of a child who is learning to spell at school and to skate after school. In skating, the child has a coach who demonstrates new moves and strategies, and who encourages the child to venture onto the ice to try them. After all, the child must be willing to try new movements.

In learning to spell, a child learns new words and strategies, and then uses this skill in spelling other words. The child's spelling coach is the teacher, who demonstrates a variety of skills and encourages the child to use them. The spelling coach ensures that the child is motivated, because in order to learn to spell, a child must be an active participant.

Conducting the Spelling Lesson

Materials for the Spelling Lesson

The basic materials required for the spelling lesson are a teacher's chalkboard; a small, individual chalkboard, eraser, and piece of chalk for each student; pencils and paper for tests (as required).

Spelling lessons last for about 20–40 minutes, depending on the size of the class and their attention span. (Attention span can vary significantly for a variety of reasons. For example, right before spring break, students may be much less focused.) Each lesson consists of three parts: Review; New Words and Strategies; New Words and Mastered Words.

Because chalkboard space is limited and smaller groups are more manageable, the class is split into smaller groups. When you are introducing a new unit, divide the class randomly into two groups for initial instruction. These two groups are always selected *at random*. This ensures that students do not feel that they have been branded as weak spellers. Another benefit is that weaker spellers in both groups get a chance to hear what strategies the students with stronger spelling skills use to remember the spelling of a word. While you work with one group, the other students can complete independent activities (math assignments, silent reading, or arts and crafts projects). Later, when you are conducting review lessons, you may want to divide the class into three groups.

> Note: Instead of chalkboards, the students could use magnetic boards and letters; or sand/salt in a tray; or individual students could work at computers with a large type size on the screen.

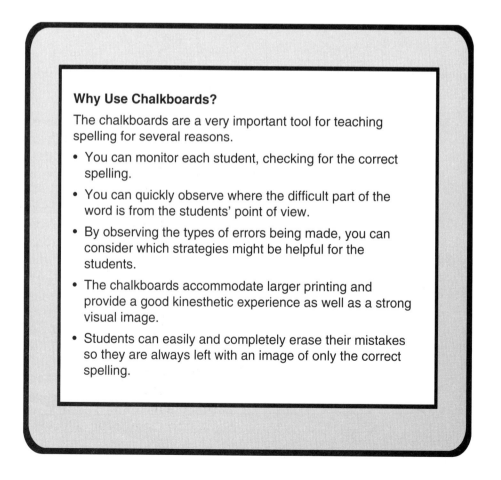

Why Use Chalkboards?

The chalkboards are a very important tool for teaching spelling for several reasons.

- You can monitor each student, checking for the correct spelling.

- You can quickly observe where the difficult part of the word is from the students' point of view.

- By observing the types of errors being made, you can consider which strategies might be helpful for the students.

- The chalkboards accommodate larger printing and provide a good kinesthetic experience as well as a strong visual image.

- Students can easily and completely erase their mistakes so they are always left with an image of only the correct spelling.

The Lesson

Part One

The first part is a review of previously learned words. This is a warm up and confidence-building session. It also provides an opportunity for informal evaluation of how well students remember the strategies and spelling patterns from earlier lessons.

Focus at least fifty percent of the lesson on reviewing previous words to ensure mastery. Students need adequate review to practise using the strategies and to develop long-term memory of the correct spelling. Rushing on to new words creates a house of cards that does not have a strong foundation for new words in the future.

What to do:

- Arrange the students in a circle around you so that you can see their chalkboards.
- Dictate a word and provide a context for it. Students should print the word on their chalkboards, starting at the top left corner. Their letters should be about five centimeters tall.
- After the students have printed the word, spell out the word correctly letter by letter. Students check their word, and this provides auditory as well as visual reinforcement of the correct spelling. Students who have made errors can erase them and rewrite the word correctly.
- Check each student's chalkboard to ensure everyone has it printed correctly.
- Discuss how individual students remembered the correct spelling.
- Ask students to erase their boards, and get ready for the next word.

Part Two

Introduce new words in this middle part of the lesson. The group uses problem solving as they discuss strategies for remembering how to spell each word. Ask the students to write down the correct spelling of the new word. Have them analyze the word to see if it is logical or tricky. (For example, if the students were learning to spell **hit** and **one**, **hit** is a logical word because all the letters represent the sounds you hear in the word. However, **one** is a tricky word because the letters do not match the sounds in the word.)

What to do:

- Introduce a new word. Dictate this word, and look for those students who already know how to spell it. Check for the kinds of errors that other students are making.
- Dictate the correct spelling of the word. When all the students have the correct spelling printed on their chalkboards, discuss the word with the group.
- Talk about the tricky part of the word — the part where students commonly made errors. Discuss how the tricky part creates

problems for remembering how to spell the word. Talk about strategies for remembering the spelling.

- Initially, use examples from the lessons in this book to provide models.
- Ask students to clear their chalkboards.

Part Three

In the final part of the lesson, students review the new words mixed in with words they have already mastered. Keep a record of which words are new and which words have already been taught. For example, students might spell two previously learned words, and then one of the new words. For each word, the students identify the strategy that they used to remember the spelling. This helps the students practise using the new strategies from their short-term memory. In the next lesson, you will be able to evaluate whether or not the strategies were effective over the longer term.

What to do:

- Dictate one of the previously learned words. Go over the correct spelling and discuss the strategies students used to remember it. Repeat this process with another already mastered word, and again, with one of the new words.
- Have the students discuss how each word can help them remember the spelling of other words. (For example, when students have mastered **big**, they can change one letter to make **dig** and **pig**.)

After about six to eight lessons, students are ready to be tested. They will have learned approximately twenty new words, and reviewed or extended their skills for up to about fifty words.

Evaluation

The goal is for each student to achieve 100% on the spelling test. However, note that another important aspect of evaluation is the students' attitude and level of confidence. Students who rarely, if ever, correctly spell all the words on a test, often see themselves as stupid, and they begin to believe that spelling is random — and something to dread. Helping these students develop strategies for remembering the correct spelling of the list words, and retesting them until they achieve 100% accuracy, demonstrates to them that they *can* learn to spell. This in turn helps them gain confidence in their ability to learn, and each new set of words gives the students a stronger foundation of words *they know* and, therefore, can use in learning to spell more new words.

It is usually clear to individual teachers when students are ready for a test. Make sure that students have had an opportunity to use several strategies for a list of words. The test is a traditional spelling test, and the number of words on a test can vary from about ten to twenty. If you choose to test ten words at a time, testing needs to be done at more frequent intervals.

Note: Initially, you may want the groups to study fewer words. You will find, however, that over the long term, students learn new words more quickly and independently as they develop confidence and the cognitive strategies for remembering how to spell words.

In many classrooms, students with weak spelling skills tend to get consistently low grades in spelling. This is likely (partly) because they never have a chance to master one list of words before the new list is introduced. These students usually have not developed the necessary mastery of initial word lists that they could apply when spelling new words. A student who misspells **come** is likely to misspell **some**, as well.

To administer the tests, have the students fold a sheet of lined paper in half vertically and write the numbers down the left side of the left margin. When they take the test, students print the words on the left side of the page and use the right side to note any strategies they used to remember how to spell each word.

To score the test, give two marks if the student spells the word correctly. Give one mark if the spelling was incorrect, but the student identifies a strategy. This encourages students to think about their spelling and to be less impulsive as they print each word. As a result, they are more likely to spell the words correctly. Some students may prefer to spell the word, then check it by writing out the strategy. Other students will want to write the strategy first, and then spell the word.

The test results will identify the students who need more instruction. You will need to create new student groupings to accommodate different students' needs. Students who spelled each word correctly can work independently on enrichment spelling words or on assignments for other subjects. Group the other students so they receive help with their specific errors. For example, students who correctly spelled 75% or more of the words get help only for the few words they misspelled. Students who spelled less than 75% of the words correctly should receive additional help over several lessons. When students who needed extra help have had some practice, retest them until they can spell all the words correctly.

Spelling Words Group 1	Speling Words Group 2	Spelling Words Group 3
gravel	dirt	dirt
because	soil	soil
sedimentary	stone	stone
igneous	rock	rock
metamorphic	speck	speck
mineral	sand	sand
planet	tin	tin
continent	jar	jar
mountain	rain	hard
boulder	hard	soft
diamond	ear	gold
volcano	spark	spark
earthquake	gold	silver
ignite	silver	flint
spark	metamorphic	ear
flint	diamond	little
quartz	earth	bone
copper	igneous	pebble
pebble	gem	sandstone
sediment	continent	tent

These spelling lists are from a Grade 3 unit about rocks. Each group has words related to the unit. Group 1 clearly has a list of more challenging words, while Group 3 is studying words that stress spelling patterns commonly learned at this grade level.

Lesson Plans

The Building Blocks for Spelling High Frequency Words...27

The Building Blocks for Spelling High Frequency Words

Basic Building Blocks

Students bring different levels of knowledge and ability to their first years of learning to read and spell. The lessons in this book assume that students have some basic building blocks as noted below. However, these building blocks are not prerequisites to learning to spell. The lessons in this book will help to develop, reinforce, and enrich these skills.

A vocabulary of basic concepts in spelling

- words; letters—first, last, and middle; consonants; and vowels

Early reading skills

- tracking
- left-to-right eye movements
- recognition of a few sight words
- beginning skills at "sounding out" words

Confidence in Printing Skills

- ability to form the letters of the alphabet.
- confidence in printing allows students to focus on the correct spelling of a word instead of how to form the letters.

Capital Letters and Lower-Case Letters

- students sometimes use both capital and lower-case letters in one word, frequently when the lower-case letter can be "reversed" (as with **b** for **d**, or **p** for **q**).
- do not mark words with both capital and lower-case letters "wrong" in the early grades.
- students will learn to incorporate capitals and lower-case letters correctly later on as a part of learning grammar.

Basic phonics skills

- a few basic phonics skills are helpful, but are not required for the lessons.
- include common consonants and blends such as **sh**, **ch**, and **th**.

Frequently used words in early reading

- basic words in early reading materials
  - a   an   at
  - go   no   so
  - he   me   she   we
  - I
  - is   it
  - the
  - to   up

A Word About Reading Skills

Teachers probably know many students who are good readers with weak spelling skills. But, how many students with good spelling skills are weak readers?

Learning to spell these tricky, high frequency words improves word recognition and fluency in a child's reading. Students who can spell a particular word can also read it. Students can apply the strategies they learn during spelling to all the other words they read in their books.

A Word About Phonics Skills

Phonics skills are one important strategy of many that help children develop good spelling skills. Phonics skills have a role in many of the spelling lessons in this book, but teachers should be aware that some students have great difficulty in understanding or recognizing the **sounds** in English. This spelling program was first developed for children who had difficulty hearing some sounds in English because of a disability or because their first language was not English.

Teachers are encouraged to use a variety of strategies to help students rather than rely on phonics alone. Note that there are several English words in which phonics skills are of no help (e.g., **one**, **does**).

Using Auditory and Visual Learning Styles as Building Blocks for Spelling

There is a distinct difference between an auditory learning style and a visual learning style. This difference is often most noticeable during spelling lessons. Auditory learners acquire knowledge through listening and remembering what they heard. Visual learners learn through seeing and remembering what they saw. Most students demonstrate a combination of auditory and visual learning styles, but every classroom will have a range of students, some who will be primarily auditory learners, and others who will be primarily visual learners.

Auditory Learners	Visual Learners
• begin to spell at a younger age	• begin to spell a later age because they need more opportunities to see a word
• are more comfortable using invented spellings when they write stories	• are not comfortable using invented spellings when they write stories
• will guess at the spelling of a word	• dislike guessing at the spelling of a word
• phonics make sense to them • phonics provide an important strategy for them	• phonics are often difficult for them • rely more on configuration, visual cues, and visualization (than on phonics)

There is often an interesting pattern in the spelling errors of visual and auditory learners. Visual learners tend to use the correct letters, but mix up the order. Auditory learners tend to use letters that represent the sounds they hear in a word.

Correct Spellings	Common Errors of Visual Learners	Common Errors of Auditory Learners
said	siad	sed
help	hlep	halp
does	dose	duz
funny	funy	funne

A Word About the Lesson Plans

Our society views good spelling skills as a sign of intelligence and competence. People with good spelling skills get higher marks, higher education, and better jobs. Helping children to develop a positive attitude towards spelling in the early years has a long-term impact on their lives. Poor spelling skills can result in underestimating a student's true potential, which can translate into missed opportunities.

The lesson plans in this book were developed to encourage children to become active, imaginative, and playful participants in learning to spell. The lesson plans demonstrate the variety of direct instruction methods and the interactions between the teacher and students. Many of the ideas for remembering how to spell certain words come from personal classroom experience — including ideas generated by the children.

The material is presented in a manner that allows teachers to observe how the lessons can be delivered in a relaxed and novel way. The methods employed in the lessons encourage student participation in discussions and problem solving.

Strategies

Word	Foundation Words	Phonics Skills or Phonemic Awareness	Visuals and Visual Cues as Memory Aids	Visualization of the Shapes of Letters and Words	Word Analysis	Word Analogy	Word Families, Patterns, Music, Rhyme, Rhythm	Spelling Probabilities	Model and Monitor the Word	Kinesthetics and Tactile Awareness	Context	Storytelling	Numeracy Skills or Math Analogy	Mnemonic
again	●	●	●						●					●
all			●	●					●					●
always	●				●				●					●
any	●	●			●				●			●		●
are	●	●			●				●				●	●
as	●	●	●						●					●
ate	●	●							●					●
because	●		●		●				●			●		●
big			●			●			●		●			●
black	●	●	●		●				●	●				●
blue		●	●				●		●					●
buy		●					●		●					●
can	●	●		●			●		●					●
come	●					●	●		●					●
cow	●	●	●						●					●
day		●							●	●		●		●
did					●				●		●			●
does	●	●			●	●			●			●		●
down	●			●	●				●			●		●
eat	●				●	●			●					●
eight		●			●				●				●	●
every	●	●							●					●
find	●	●	●		●				●					●
first		●	●		●			●	●					●
four			●	●					●			●		●
from	●	●	●		●				●		●			●
funny	●		●	●					●		●	●	●	●
give					●				●		●	●		●
good			●	●					●		●	●	●	●
has	●	●	●		●				●					●
have		●	●		●				●		●			●
head		●	●	●	●				●					●

Strategies

Word	Foundation Words	Phonics Skills or Phonemic Awareness	Visuals and Visual Cues as Memory Aids	Visualization of the Shapes of Letters and Words	Word Analysis	Word Analogy	Word Families, Patterns, Music, Rhyme, Rhythm	Spelling Probabilities	Model and Monitor the Word	Kinesthetics and Tactile Awareness	Context	Storytelling	Numeracy Skills or Math Analogy	Mnemonic
help	●		●	●	●				●			●		●
here	●				●				●		●	●		●
jump	●		●	●					●					●
know	●		●		●	●			●				●	●
little	●	●			●				●	●		●	●	●
look		●	●		●	●			●					●
new	●		●	●					●					●
once	●	●	●	●					●			●		●
one	●	●			●				●				●	●
our, out		●	●		●			●	●			●		●
pull			●						●		●	●		●
said	●	●						●	●		●			●
saw			●	●					●		●	●		●
seven, eleven	●				●		●		●				●	●
soon	●	●	●		●		●		●					●
there	●		●		●	●			●		●			●
they	●				●	●			●		●			●
three	●				●	●	●		●				●	●
two			●	●					●			●		●
walk					●				●		●			●
want	●				●				●					●
were	●	●			●				●		●			●
what	●				●				●					●
when	●		●		●				●			●		●
where	●		●		●				●		●			●
which			●						●		●			●
white	●	●			●				●			●		●
who									●		●			●
would, should, could		●			●				●					●
you	●		●					●	●		●			●
your	●		●		●				●		●			●

again

Foundation word rain
Target word again
Common error agen

Instructional sequence of words

rain
gain
again

New words

main, pain, vain
slain
brain, drain, train
stain

Discussion	Strategies
• Spell **rain**.	• Use the foundation word.
• Discuss how the letter **i** makes the letter **a** say its name. Point out that this is different from the usual pattern of adding an **e** to the end of the word.	• Develop phonemic awareness.
• Students may find it easier to remember the **i** in rain if they think of a raindrop that runs down a windowpane.	• Use a visual aid.
• Change one letter to spell **gain**.	
• Add one letter to spell **again**.	
• Look at the word in context, and develop a mnemonic.	• Use a mnemonic.

Sample Mnemonic	Your Mnemonic
I hope it will **rain again**. rain gain a + gain = again	

all

Foundation word   (not applicable)

Target word   all

Common error   ol

Instructional sequence of words

all

New words

ball, call, fall, hall, mall, tall, wall small

Discussion	Strategies
• Use a question-answer format to discuss what students carry in their pencil cases. Accept all reasonable answers (e.g., pens, ruler, eraser, pencils, crayons), and then focus on pencils.	• Develop phonemic awareness.
• Show the students two new pencils, and one that is approximately half that length. Tell them, "These are **all** my pencils." Print the word **all** on the board, using standard primary letter characters.	• Use a visual aid.
• Ask students to look at the word **all** carefully. Can they see where the letters have pencils in them? (See the visual on this page.) Use the stick in the letter **a** to make a short pencil, the sticks of the two letters **ll** to make two long pencils.	
• Ask students how thinking about this picture could help them remember how to spell **all**. Some students may associate three letters in **all** and three pencils. One of the letters has a short pencil [**a**], and two letters are tall [**ll**].	• Use visual cues
• With the students, develop a mnemonic for the word **all**.	• Use a mnemonic.

Sample Mnemonic	Your Mnemonic
I have **all** my pencils.	

always

Foundation words **day, say**

Target word **always**

Common error **olwaz**

Instructional sequence of words

day

say

way ways always

Discussion	Strategies
• Spell **day** and **say**. (See the lesson for the word **day**.)	• Use the foundation words.
• Change one letter to spell **way**. Add one letter to spell **ways**.	
• Talk about getting lost, perhaps in the woods. When you don't know where you're going, it is **always** good to have someone with you who knows where they are going.	• Use storytelling.
• Print **always** on the board. Have the students look at the word, then ask them, "Can anyone find the name of someone who always knows the way?" (Al always knows the way.)	• Encourage observation.
• Students spell **always**.	
• Develop a mnemonic phrase that associates **Al**, **always**, and **way**.	• Develop a mnemonic.

Sample Mnemonic	Your Mnemonic
Al always knows the **way**.	

Al always knows the way!

34

any

Foundation words and, ant

Target words any

Common errors eny

Instructional sequence of words

and   ant   any

New words

many

anyone (enrichment)

anybody (enrichment)

Discussion	Strategies
• Invite the students to print **and**.	• Use the foundation words.
• Ask the group to change one letter in **and** to spell **ant**.	
• Ask the students to make the word **any** by changing just one letter in the word **ant**. Let them do the reasoning for changing the **t** to a **y**. (The tricky part of **any** is the initial vowel sound, which is not spelled the way it sounds. It sounds as though it should start with **en**.)	• Discuss phonemic differences. • Use problem solving.
• Print **ant** on the chalkboard. As review, ask the students how to change **ant** to **any**.	• Use word analysis.
• With input from the children, make up a story that uses the words **and**, **ant**, and **any**. A sample follows. Yip was an anteater. His favorite food was **ants**. One day he ate a real **ant and** a chocolate **ant**. He really liked the chocolate one. He went to the store. "Do you have **any** chocolate **ants**?" asked Yip. "I'm sorry," said the clerk. "We don't have any chocolate ones today. Just strawberry."	• Use storytelling to develop a mnemonic.
Sample Mnemonic **Y**ip asked, "Do you have **any** chocolate **ant**s?" 	**Your Mnemonic**

are

Foundation words   car

Target word   are

Common error   ar, r

Instructional sequence of words   New words

car

are

Discussion	Strategies
• Use the word **car** in a discussion. Invite the students to spell the word **car**. Print **car** on the chalkboard.	• Use the foundation word **car**.
• Ask the students what sound is made by the letters **ar** in **car**.	• Apply phonemic awareness.

• Under **car**, print the word **are** on the board. Talk about how both **car** and **are** have three letters. To make **car** into **are**, they need to erase one letter, and then add one letter. Show them
 	
       car
        ar
      ar + e = are
 	
Count the letters in **are**.
	• Use mathematics (number of letters), and word analogy.

• Develop a mnemonic that uses the foundation word and the target.	• Develop a mnemonic.
Sample Mnemonic We **are** going in the **car**. 	**Your Mnemonic**

as

Foundation words   is

Target word   as

Common error   az

Instructional sequence of words

is

as

New words

has (word analogy)
was (phonemic awareness, word analogy)

Discussion	Strategies
• Invite the students to spell **is**. • Change one letter to spell **as**. • Ask the students what they hear at the end of this word. Point out that the letter s can make an /s/ or a /z/ sound. • Have the children imagine walking along a trail and seeing a snake. (Print the word **as** on the board, making the **s** look like a snake.) Ask the children, "Where is the snake?"	• Use the foundation word **is**. • Use phonemic awareness. • Use storytelling and a visual aid. • Develop a mnemonic that that uses the word and the visual aid.
Sample Mnemonic **As** I was walking, I saw **a s**nake. 	**Your Mnemonic**

ate

Foundation words   at

Target word   ate

Common error   aet

Instructional sequence of words

at   ate

New words

date, fate, gate, hate, late, mate
plate, slate
[crate, grate, create, inflate,
deflate (enrichment only)]

Discussion	Strategies
Note: The following strategy can also be used for **eat**, the present tense of eat. It is very important that students learn these **ate** and **eat** words in different lessons with a good length of time in between.	
• Have the group print **at** on their boards. Then begin a brief question and answer dialogue with the students.	• Use the foundation word.
You: "I **ate** supper **at** home last night. Where did you eat supper?"	
Student: "McDonald's."	
[Someone will probably have gone to McDonald's, or will provide an appropriate sentence fragment such as "My grandmother's."]	
You: "You **ate** McDonald's?"	
Student: "**At** McDonald's. I ate **at** McDonald's."	
[Students will usually correct themselves.]	
• Explain that wherever they ate supper, they ate **at** a place: **at** McDonald's, **at** Grandma's house, **at** the table.	• Use the foundation and target words in context.
• Ask students to look at their boards. What letter could they add to make the **a** in **at** say its name? What word does that make? [**at** + **e** = **ate**] Help the group develop a mnemonic that associates **at** and **ate**.	• Use phonemic awareness. • Develop a mnemonic that that uses the word and the visual aid.
Sample Mnemonic	**Your Mnemonic**

We **ate at E**d's house.

Where did you eat?

We ate at Ed's house.

38

because

Foundation words: be, car, use

Target word: because

Common error: becuz

Instructional sequence of words

because — be, [car], us, use

Discussion	Strategies
• Show students a picture of a big bear in the wild. Imagine a big bear driving a car. Ask them, "Do you think this could really happen? Why or why not?"	• Use the foundation words and a visual aid.
• Print **because** on the board.	
• Help students to identify smaller words in **because** that do not require changing any letters (**be**, **us**, **use**). **Note:** The word **cause** is a difficult word for young students. Few will be able to see it as a "word within a word" in **because**. Instead, introduce the word **car**, and continue the lesson, using the following strategies. Add the word **car** to the lesson, so it can be used with the story below.	• Word analysis: chunk the word.
• Use the smaller words in a story. Use the last line of the story as the mnemonic phrase. Have you ever seen a bear driving a **car**? Bears are not good drivers. Why would a bear **be** driving a car? Uh-oh! There might be an accident because of this! He might bump the car into **us because** he doesn't know how to **use** the brakes. Bear, bear! **Use** the brakes! Bump! The bear bumped the car **because** he didn't **use** the brakes.	• Use storytelling to develop a mnemonic.

• On the board, follow the word sequence **be + car + use**. Some students might benefit from the mental image of the car bumping into us because the bear didn't use the brakes. When the car bumps into us, it loses its **r**.
 	
    be + car + use
    be ca use
        [r̶]	

Sample Mnemonic The bear bumped the car **because** he did not **use** the brakes.	

big

Foundation words   (not applicable)

Target word   big

Common error   beg, bag

Instructional sequence of words

big

New words

dig, fig, pig, rig, wig
swig, twig
trigger (enrichment)

Discussion	Strategies
Note: Big is a tricky word. Some youngsters have difficulty hearing the vowel sound correctly, and this results in the common misspelling **beg**.	
• Ask if anyone has gone fishing. When you go fishing, you hope to catch a **big** fish. How **big** was the fish they caught?	• Provide a context.
• Use pictures of a fishing rod to make an analogy between the letters in **big** and the parts of the rod. Tell the group that the letter **b** is the bait. Print **b** on the board. Next, tell them that the letter **i** is the line, and its dot is the sinker. You may want to refer to the visuals or the real fishing rod again. Print **i** on the classroom chalkboard. Add **g** to make the word **big**. The letter **g** is the hook. Erase the chalkboard. Ask if everyone in the group is ready to catch a **big** fish. Have students spell **big** on their own boards. Remind them to make sure they have the "bait, line and sinker, and hook."	• Use a visual cue and an analogy to the letters in the word.
• Develop a simple mnemonic related to the context. The word "**I**" in the phrase will help them remember the letter **i** in the word.	• Use the context, the visuals, and the analogy to develop a mnemonic.
Sample Mnemonic **I** want to catch a **big** fish!	**Your Mnemonic**

black

Foundation words	make, bake, back
Target word	black
Common error	blak

Instructional sequence of words

make   bake   back   black

New words

lack, pack, rack, sack, tack
clack, slack

Discussion	Strategies
• Remind students that a vowel either says its name or a sound.	• Use phonemic awareness and previous spelling and language knowledge.
• Print **make** on the board. Review why **a** says its name in **make** [the **e** at the end]. Have students change a letter to spell **bake**.	• Use the foundation words.
• Print **back** then read it aloud with the class. Explain that **a** needs two body guards to protect the sound it makes. Invite the students to print back on the chalkboard, and underline **c** and **k**. Tell the group that with these two body guards, nothing can make **a** say its name.	• Use word analysis; change a letter. • Use a visual.
• Have the students practice spelling **bake** and **lack** in a random sequence to see if they hear the difference and know when to use **ck** and when to use **k**.	• Use word analysis; phonemic awareness.
• Ask students to spell **black**. Everyone say **black**. Check the position of the tongue when you say the beginning of the word. The tongue is on the back of the front teeth. This position indicates that an **l** is in the word. Use the story to develop a mnemonic.	• Develop a mnemonic.
Sample Mnemonic **Bake** it until it is **black**.	**Your Mnemonic**

41

blue

Foundation words (not applicable)

Target word **blue**

Common error **bloo, blu, bleu**

Instructional sequence of words

Sue   blue

New words

clue, glue

Discussion	Strategies
• Tell the students that the vowel **u** says its name if an **e** follows it. Give an example such as, "**S**ue used **glue** to stick down the picture."	• Use phonemic awareness and previous spelling and language knowledge.
• Ask the group to say **blue**. Have them check where their tongue is when they say the **l**. (It is on the back of their upper teeth). Ask for other words with –**l**. When you say **l**, your tongue is always at the back of the upper teeth.	• Use kinesthetics and emphasize pronunciation.
• Develop a mnemonic that students can associate with a vivid mental picture. For example, "**S**ue felt **blue** when she fell in bl**ue** gl**ue**." (Discuss the meaning of the first "blue" — a feeling of sadness.) **Note:** Tell students who are having difficulty hearing the **u** sound that the letter **u** is the only vowel shaped like a container, which could hold "glue."	• Use a mnemonic and a visual.
Sample Mnemonic **S**ue felt **blue** when she fell in the **glue**.	**Your Mnemonic**

buy

Foundation words   (not applicable)

Target word   buy

Common error   bi, by

Instructional sequence of words

buy

New words

guy
buy, by (word analysis,
word analogy)

Discussion	Strategies
• To elicit the concept of buying something, invite students to describe a shopping trip. Ask questions such as "Why do you go to a store? What do you do there? Do you ever see things you would like? What do you say to your mom or dad?" (Will you **buy** this for me?)	
• Have the students spell **buy**. Print it on the board correctly.	• Use phonics and rhyming words.
• Discuss the tricky parts of the word: the letter **u** in the middle, and the letter **y** at the end.	
• The letter **u** is silent. It suggests who we want to buy the item. (**u** = **you**, not me.) The letter **y** sounds like **i**. Discuss other words with **y**-endings that sound like **i** (e.g., cry, shy, try).	• Use word analysis. • Use rhyme.
• Develop a mnemonic phrase that helps students remember the letters **u** and **y**. In the sample below, **you** sounds like the letter **u**, and **y** is the first letter in the word **you**.	• Develop a mnemonic.

Sample Mnemonic	Your Mnemonic
Will **you buy** this for me?	

can

Foundation words **an**

Target word **can**

Common error **kan**

Instructional sequence of words

an   **can**

New words

ban, Dan, fan, man, pan, ran, tan
van, bran, Stan
Canada, candy [for enrichment only]

Discussion	Strategies
• Tell students that the letter **c** can make two sounds. One sound is the /**k**/ in cat; and the other sound is the /**s**/ in cent.	• Use the foundation word.
• Print **can** and **kan** on the chalkboard.	
• Draw an outline around **kan** and **can**. Discuss the shapes that the outlines make.	• Use phonics and rhyming words.
• Notice that the shape of **can** is like the shape of a can lying on its side.	• Use letter/word configuration.
• The letter **a** looks like the top of a can. The stick on **a** looks like a can opener attached to the can.	
• You could also point out that the shape of **kan** does *not* look like a **can**. The **k** makes it too tall on the left side.	
• Ask the students to print the word **can** on their boards. Then develop a mnemonic that uses an association between the shape of the word and the shape of its letters.	• Use a mnemonic.

Sample Mnemonic	Your Mnemonic
I **can** open the **can**.	

come

Foundation words **to, me**

Target word **come**

Common errors **cum, kum**

Instructional sequence of words

to   me

       come

New words

some
welcome (enrichment)

Discussion	Strategies
• Ask students to help you spell **to** and **me** on the board.	• Use the foundation words.
• Compare the spelling of **to me** and **come** with the students.	• Use word analysis, word analogy.
• Change one letter in **to me** to spell **come**.	• Use problem solving.
• Have students develop a mnemonic. It could be simple, "**Come** to me." Alternatively, you could develop a more visually oriented mnemonic that includes a memorable object or subject: "Make the dog **come** to me."	• Use a mnemonic.

Sample Mnemonic	Your Mnemonic
Make the dog **come** to me. Come to me!	

45

Foundation words (not applicable)

Target word   cow

Common error   cou, kow

Instructional sequence of words

cow

New words

bow, how, now, pow, vow

Discussion	Strategies
• **Cow** is an important foundation word for words such as **down**, **brown**, **crown**, and **frown**.	
• Use a visual technique to help students remember the spelling of this word. When letters are arranged in the correct sequence from top to bottom, they can form the picture of a cow. (See the visual on this page.)	• Use a visual; use the letters to create a visual image.
• The **c** looks like a cow's horns, the **o** is the cow's head, and the **w** makes the cow's legs.	• Use a mnemonic associated with the visual representation of the word.
Sample Mnemonic Can you draw a **cow**? 	**Your Mnemonic**

day

Foundation word   (not applicable)

Target word   day

Common error   da, dae

Instructional sequence of words

letter y   day

New words

bay, gay, hay, hooray, jay, lay, may
nay, pay, ray, say, way, away, always
clay, play, slay
bray, crayon, fray, gray, pray, tray
stray

Discussion	Strategies
• (**Note**: **day** is an important foundation word that students will use frequently.)	
• Ask students what they do when they wake up and begin a new **day**. How many wake up and stretch before they get out of bed?	• Develop phonemic awareness.
• Invite the students to pretend they are stretching at the start of a new **day**. They will follow your lead if you demonstrate stretching your arms above your head so your body forms a letter y. Encourage students to observe that they look like a letter. Which letter? (Really exaggerate it if they do not see it.)	• Use a real-life story or example.
• Print **day** on the board. Tell students that the letter **y** makes the letter **a** say its name. Develop a mnemonic based on the stretching activity: As students say a sentence with the word **day**, they can stretch out their arms to make the letter **y**.	• Use kinetic activity to emphasize the last letter. • Use a mnemonic.

Sample Mnemonic	Your Mnemonic
What a beautiful **day**!	

Foundation words (not applicable)

Target word **did**

Common error **ded**

Instructional sequence of words

did

New words

bid, hid, kid, lid
skid, slid, grid

Discussion	Strategies
Note: The word **did** can challenge students who have trouble recognizing different vowel sounds. This lesson emphasizes the **i**.	
• Ask questions that elicit the response, **I did**. Include some "surprise questions."	• Use the word in context.
• Who ate breakfast today?	
• Who had orange juice?	
• Who ate their math book?	
• Who went to bed last night?	
• Who went for recess today?	
• Who had 20 donuts for lunch?	
• Who had chocolate milk?	
• Who spilled their chocolate milk?	
Children usually enjoy confessing to all these deeds, so repeat the questions or add more to give the group further opportunities to say, "**I did**."	
• Explain that the person who did all these things is in the word **did**. "**I did**." Ask a few more questions so students can answer, "**I did**." Have the students print **did** on their boards. Develop a mnemonic with the group.	• Use word analysis. • Develop a mnemonic.
Sample Mnemonic Who **did** this? **I did**.	**Your Mnemonic**

does

Foundation words **Joe**

Target word **does**

Common error **duz, dose**

Instructional sequence of words

Joe [Jo + e]
Joes
does

New words

doe

Discussion	Strategies
Note: In this lesson, the students use a word that does not really exist the way it is spelled in the lesson. Students in this age group are not concerned about and do not really recognize or understand the concept that an apostrophe is used in most possessives. Thus, "Joes" (Joe + s) is not problematic for them.	
• Print the name **Joe** on the board. Explain that when we spell this name for a boy or man, it has an **e** at the end. The **e** makes the **o** say its name.	• Use the foundation word. • Word analysis; word analogy. • Apply phonemic awareness.
• Ask students to add a letter to make the word say "**Joe + s.**"	
• Print **does** on the board. Ask a student to read it out loud. Ask why it is a tricky word. (It is not spelled the way it sounds.)	
• Use **Joe**, and **Joes** in context. My friend **Joe** has a computer. He can play games on it. I don't have games on my computer, but **Joe's does**.	• Use storytelling.
• Develop a simple mnemonic.	• Use a mnemonic.

Sample Mnemonic	Your Mnemonic
"My computer doesn't work, but **Joe[']s does**." My computer doesn't work but **Joe's** does.	

down

Foundation words   cow

Target word   down

Common error   don, doun

Instructional sequence of words

cow   down

         brown

New words

gown, town, clown
crown, drown, frown

Discussion	Strategies
• Review the spelling of **cow**. • Show students that cow is part of the word **down**, except that cow is hidden. The **c** is part of the **d**. • Then, discuss ways to remember the **n**. One way is to think of the **n** as a hill. You can develop a mnemonic about a cow going down a hill.	• Use the foundation word. • Use word analysis. • Use visualizing letters and letter construction. • Use a mnemonic.
Sample Mnemonic The cow ran **down** the hill.	**Your Mnemonic**

eat

Foundation words **at**

Target word **eat**

Common error **et, eet**

Instructional sequence of words

at   eat

New words

beat, feat, heat, meat, neat, seat

Discussion	Strategies
• Say the word **eat** and ask the students to print the first sound they hear in the word.	
• Ask the group, "Where do people **eat**?" Answers will vary, but try to elicit a good number of phrases with **at** (e.g., We eat **at** Grandma's house. We eat **at** a restaurant. We eat **at** the table.	• Use word analysis; chunking and adding parts.
• Ask the students to print **at** beside the letter for the first sound in **eat**. They now have the word **eat**.	• Use the foundation word.
• Help the students see that the correct spelling of **eat** reminds us that we **eat at** a particular place.	• Use a mnemonic.

Sample Mnemonic	Your Mnemonic
We **eat at** the table.	

51

eight

Foundation words (letters) a, b, c, d, e, f, g, h

Target word eight

Common error ate

Instructional sequence of words

abcdefgh
efgh
efght
eight

New words

eighty (enrichment)
weighty (enrichment)

Discussion	Strategies
• Ask students to print the first eight letters of the alphabet: 　　**a b c d e f g h** • Ask students, "What number added to itself makes 8?" (4 + 4 = 8) On the board, cross out the first four letters: 　　**a̶ b̶ c̶ d̶ e f g h** Look at the letters that are left. Ask students to add the letter that makes the last sound in the word **eight**. 　　**e f g h + t** • Cut the top off of **f**, which makes it look like **i**, and now the word spells **eight**. • Review and summarize the process to develop a mnemonic.	• Use word analysis; phonemic awareness • Use mathematics. • Use a mnemonic.
Sample Mnemonic Print the first **eight** letters of the alphabet.	**Your Mnemonic**

every

Foundation words **eve, ever, very**

Target word **every**

Common error **evry**

Instructional sequence of words

eve

ever   very   every

New words

even

everything (enrichment)

everybody (enrichment)

everyone (enrichment)

Discussion	Strategies
• Talk about the words **night**, **evening**, and **eve** and their similar meanings. (You could also note that Eve is a woman's name.)	• Chunk the word; add letters.
• Have students print **eve**. Ask questions such as, "What is New Year's **Eve**? Do you **ever** stay up **very** late, until midnight, on New Year's **Eve**?"	• Use a mnemonic.
• Ask students to add a letter to make **eve** into **ever**.	• Discuss pronunciation.
• **eve** + **r** = **ever**	
• And then add one more letter to spell **every**.	
• **ever** + **y** = **every**	• Chunk the word.
• (Also, **e** + **very** = **every**)	
• Develop a mnemonic using ever and every (e.g., Do you **ever** watch **every** cartoon on Saturday?)	• Use a mnemonic.
• Have students look at the word that is left if they cover the first letter **e** in **every** (**very**).	
• Develop a mnemonic that helps students associate the four words **eve**, **ever**, **very** and **every**.	
Sample Mnemonic **Eve** is **very** careful **every** time she prints **ever**. eve ever very every	**Your Mnemonic**

find

Foundation words	in
Target word	find
Common error	finde, fined

Instructional sequence of words

in   f + in + d

New words

bind, hind, kind, mind, rind, wind

Discussion	Strategies
The tricky part of **find** is that the **i** says its name. Some students also have difficulty hearing the nasal n-sound.	
• Ask students to spell **in**. Then have them add the first sound in the word **find**.	• Use phonemic awareness; word analysis.
f + in	
• Now ask the students to add the last sound from **find**.	
f + in + d = find	
• Use find in a memorable context. For example, ask the group where pirates hide their treasure. You should get answers such as, "Pirates hide their treasure **in** caves, **in** chests, **in** the sand…" The emphasis is on **in** because **in** is the foundation for **find**.	• Use a visual with the discussion.
• Ask, "Where would we look if we wanted to **find** treasure?" (We would look **in** something.)	• Use a mnemonic.
• Develop a mnemonic to help students associate **find** with the foundation word **in**.	

Sample Mnemonic	Your Mnemonic
We will **find** the treasure **in** the chest.	

first

Foundation words   (not applicable)

Target word   first

Common error   ferst, furst

Instructional sequence of words

-er words (teacher, farmer, dancer)
-ur- and -ir- words (burn, bird)
first

New words

thirst

Discussion	Strategies
• Talk about the sound made by **-er** in words that end with **-er** (e.g., teach**er**, farm**er**, danc**er**).	• Use phonemic awareness; word analysis.
• Explain that the same **-er** sound is usually spelled by **-ur** or **-ir** in the middle of words. The sound is sometimes in the middle of these words (e.g., b**ur**n, b**ir**d).	• Discuss the "spelling probability."
• Say "**first**" and ask students where they hear the **-er** sound. Have students print the word on their boards, and underline the letters that make the **-er** sound. (Print **first** on the board.) Discuss which **-er** sound it is. (It's **-ir-** because, "**I** want to be **first**.")	
• Use **first** in a mnemonic sentence.	• Use a mnemonic.

Sample Mnemonic	Your Mnemonic
I want to be the **first**.	

four

Foundation words (not applicable)

Target word **four**

Common error **for, fore**

Instructional sequence of words

four

New words

Discussion	Strategies
• Print **four** on the chalkboard. Ask the students to count the number of letters. There are 4 letters in the word **four**.	• Use a mathematical analogy.
• Explain that the middle two letters are the tricky part of the word. Tell the students a story that connects the letters and their shapes to the actual word. You can try the following story, or have students contribute to a class story. Show the letters **f**, **o**, **u**, and **r** as you tell the following story.	• Use storytelling.
The other day I went to a bakery and had some hot chocolate and a doughnut. The doughnuts looked so good, I decided to eat **four**. "F o u r, **four**," I thought. "Wow! The **f** looks like a person carrying a tray. It could be me!" Then I thought, "The letter **o** is like a doughnut." I sat down to eat, and I dunked my doughnut in my hot chocolate. "The letter **u** is like a mug!" When I finished eating all **four** doughnuts, my hands were really sticky, so I had to wash them. That's when I noticed that the tap looked like **r**, the last letter in **four** — **f o u r**.	• Identify letter shapes and visual cues.
• Develop a mnemonic with the group.	• Use a mnemonic.

Sample Mnemonic	Your Mnemonic
I ate **four** doughnuts. If you dunk **four** doughnuts you will need to wash at the tap.	

from

Foundation words **Tom**

Target word **from**

Common error **frum**

Instructional sequence of words

Tom   from

New words

Discussion	Strategies
• Introduce the concept of sending and receiving letters and cards, noting that you *send* a letter **to** someone, and *receive* a letter **from** someone.	• Develop a context.
• Bring in examples of letters or cards that illustrate the idea of **to** and **from**.	• Use visuals.
• Ask students to spell the name **Tom**.	
• Print **from** on the board. Ask students to identify the letters that are the same in both words.	• Use phonemic awareness; word analysis.
• Talk about the tricky part of from (the **-u** sound is made by the letter **o**). Ask students how Tom would sign a card or letter? (**from Tom**) (If possible, bring in a large card or letter that is addressed to you and signed "**from Tom**.")	
• How can this help you remember the spelling of **from**?	• Use a mnemonic.

Sample Mnemonic	Your Mnemonic
The letter is **from Tom**. To my friend, It is fun here. We have done lots of new things. We are leaving for home tomorrow. I will see you soon. From Tom ADDRESS: _____ _____ _____ _____	

funny

Foundation words   fun
Target word   funny
Common error   funne, funy

Instructional sequence of words

fun   funny

New words

bunny, sunny

Discussion	Strategies
• Have the students print **u** on their boards. Ask them what letter it makes if they turn their boards around. (The **u** becomes **n**.) Now have them try it with **un**.	• Develop a context. • Use letter configuration and visuals.
• Briefly explain that twins are two things that are the same, and triplets are three things that are the same. Print the letters **f nnn y** and **f unn y** on the chalkboard. Tell the students these letters are the "funny family." Point out the triplets in **f nnn y**. Ask what one of the triplets is doing in **f unn y**? (Standing on its head.) Now tell the students this story.	• Use numeracy: twins = 2; triplets = 3. • Use storytelling.
A photographer was trying to take some pictures of the **funny** family. Every time the photographer was ready, one of the triplets kept doing something **funny**. What could that be? The photographer came out from behind his camera. He walked over to the triplets. "Very **funny**!" he said, as he turned the triplet over to stand up with the others. Before he got back to his camera, the triplet had done a somersault and was upside down again. And that's why the family is called the **funny** family.	
• Develop a mnemonic associated with the word structure.	• Use a mnemonic.
Sample Mnemonic One of the triplets is acting **funny**. 	**Your Mnemonic**

give

Foundation words   (not applicable)

Target word   give

Common error   giv

Instructional sequence of words

give

New words

live

Discussion	Strategies
• See if students have played or watched team sports. Ask if anyone has watched a game where the crowd yelled out cheers for the teams. Talk about "cheerleaders." Elicit some examples of cheers. If students don't know any, suggest some easy ones (e.g., "Go, Leafs, go!" and "Give me a **g**! Give me an **o**! What have you got? **GO! Go**, team, **go**!")	• Develop a context.
• Tell the following story about a group of cheerleaders:	• Use storytelling.

The cheerleaders for a school team were glum. They wanted the crowd to shout the word give, but their cheer never worked. They shouted, "Give me a **g**! Give me an **i**! Give me a **v**! What have you got?" The crowd was silent. What was wrong?
    The cheerleaders tried one more time. They yelled, "Give me a **g**! Give me an **i**! Give me a **v**! What have you got?" and someone in the crowd yelled back, "Nothing. You need an **e**! **g-i-v-e**! **Give**!"
    The cheerleaders looked at each other, looked at the crowd, and then yelled: "Give me a **g**! Give me an **i**! Give me a **v**! Give me an **e**! What have you got?" "**Give**!" shouted the crowd.	

• Print **give** on the board, and discuss its tricky part. The **i** does not say its own name, even though there is an **e** at the end of the word.	• Use word analysis.
• Develop a mnemonic based on the story.	• Use a mnemonic.

Sample Mnemonic	Your Mnemonic
Give me an **e**! 	

59

good

Foundation words   (not applicable)

Target word   good

Common error   god, gud

Instructional sequence of words

oooo gooo good

New words

wood

Discussion	Strategies
• Develop a context for the word **good**. Talk about cookies, a favorite subject for most young children. Ask "What is your favorite kind of cookie?"	• Develop a context.
• Draw one cookie on the board. Tell the students one cookie is "okay." But two would be better. Draw a second cookie on the board. "Well, three cookies are fine." Add another cookie on the board. "But four," (draw a fourth cookie) "are **good**."	• Use storytelling.
• Now you have four cookies (circles) on the board. Show the group how to make the four cookies into the word good by adding the hook for the **g**, and the stick for the **d**. As you make the word, repeat the story: One cookie is okay. But two cookies are better. Well three cookies are fine. But four cookies are good.	• Look at word and letter configuration; visual cues.
• Ask the students to print **good** on their boards, and add dots where there are nuts and chocolate chips in the cookies.	
• Develop a mnemonic for the correct spelling.	• Use a mnemonic.

Sample Mnemonic	Your Mnemonic
These cookies are **good**.	

Foundation words hat, as

Target word has

Common error haz

Instructional sequence of words

New words

hat   has

Discussion	Strategies
• Briefly discuss "magicians" and "magic tricks." Ask students what a magician usually pulls out of his hat (a rabbit).	
• Tell the following story about a magician who didn't pull a rabbit out of his hat!	• Use storytelling.
Presto the magician could make coins appear and disappear. He could change white scarves into white birds. But he couldn't pull a rabbit from his **hat**! One day at a birthday party, Presto tried to pull a rabbit from his **hat**. Suddenly all the children screamed and ran away from him. Poor Presto! When he looked at the big hairy spider he had pulled out of his **hat**, he screamed and ran away, too!	
• Print **is**, **as**, and **was** on the board. Ask students what the last *sound* in each word is. Then ask what letter makes the **-z** sound in these words.	• Apply phonemic awareness.
• Ask the students to print **hat**. Tell them to change one letter to make the word **has**.	• Use the foundation word **hat**. Use word analysis; change a letter.
• Develop a mnemonic with the students that reminds them that **has** ends with **s**. (Presto's **hat has** a big hairy spider.)	• Use a mnemonic.
• An alternative idea is to use the word **as**, add an **h** to make **has**.	• Use the foundation word **as**. Use phonemic awareness; rhyme.

Sample Mnemonic	**Your Mnemonic**
Presto's **hat has** a big hairy spider.	

have

Foundation words (not applicable)

Target word   have

Common error   hav

Instructional sequence of words

have

New words

Discussion	Strategies
• Print **have** on the board. Talk about the sound the letter **a** makes. This is the tricky part because even though there is an **e** at the end of the word, the letter **a** does not say its own name.	• Use phonemic awareness.
• Ask the students what they ate for breakfast. Talk about why we eat cereal, milk, and fruit juice. (All these foods provide vitamins and minerals that are good for us.)	• Use word analysis. • Provide a context.
• Ask students to identify the sound that is at the beginning of *vitamin*. Tell the students that the names of the different vitamins are usually letters of the alphabet. Print **vitamin E** on the chalkboard.	• Use phonemic awareness.
• Discuss how the first two letters and sounds in **have** are logical. Point out that if the students print **ha** and then think of **vitamin E** they can spell **have**.	
• Develop a mnemonic with the group to help them make the connection between **vitamin E** and the spelling of **have**.	• Develop a mnemonic to establish a connection between the sounds, words, and letters.

Sample Mnemonic	Your Mnemonic
Did you **have** **v**itamin **E** today? Did you **have** vitamin E today?	

head

Foundation words   (not applicable)

Target word   head

Common error   hed

Instructional sequence of words

head

New words

ahead

Discussion	Strategies
Note: "**head**" is an important foundation word for teaching **read**. • In large printing write **h e a d**. (Be sure to use standard primary chalkboard printing.) • Go over the spelling letter by letter. • Suggest that the **a** looks a head in profile, with long hair at the back. When you say **a**, draw a face in profile in the **a**. Then print the **d**. • Now direct students to look at the "head" in the word **head**. Ask if it is a boy's head or a girl's head. Look at the word for a clue. (It is a boy's head because the first two letters spell **he**.) This visual cue can help students to remember that **a** comes after the **e** in h**ea**d.	• Use a mnemonic. • Use phonemic awareness. • Use word analysis. • Develop observation skills. • Use a visual cue.
Sample Mnemonic **He** has lost his **head**. 	**Your Mnemonic**

help

Foundation words **he**

Target word **help**

Common error **halp, hlep**

Instructional sequence of words

he   help

New words

kelp (enrichment)

Discussion	Strategies
• **Help** is a difficult word because of the vowel sound. Some students may not be able to differentiate between the sound of an **a** versus an **e** in the word. Use a story to help students remember the sequence of the letters. Some students will benefit if the story helps them to associate the configuration of the letters.	
• "Help! Someone, please help me!" shouted the boy. He looked up the side of a high, steep cliff. He called out "Help!" again. He couldn't see who was at the top of the cliff, but someone had heard him. A rope was slowly sliding down toward the boy. He grabbed the rope and used it to **help** him climb up the side of the cliff. "I wonder who brought the rope to help me. Was it a man or a woman?"	• Use storytelling.
• Print **help** on the board. Ask the students what part of **help** gives a clue about who brought the rope. (Print **he** on the board, then ask the students what letter could be the rope (**l**). Add the **l** to the **he** (**hel**). Now ask the group to identify the last letter in **help**. Add **p** to spell **help**. Show them that the letter **p** looks like someone who has climbed to the top of the rope.	• Use the foundation word, then use word analysis.
• Develop a mnemonic phrase, and point out the letters in **help** that are associated with specific parts of the mnemonic phrase.	• Develop a mnemonic.
Sample Mnemonic He used a rope to **help** the boy. Help! Help!	**Your Mnemonic**

here

Foundation words   her
Target word   here
Common error   hear, hare

Instructional sequence of words   New words
her   here

Discussion	Strategies
• Ask students to spell **her**. • Establish a relationship between **her** and the **e** at the end of **here**. Tell a story about a girl named Emily (or other name beginning with **E** that is familiar to the students). Emily has lost the first letter (**E**) from her name. People are calling her **mily**. She is very upset. Her name is **E**mily, not **mily**. She soon asks everyone to search for the lost **e**. Finally, someone says, "I found it. I found **her e**. It's right **here**." • Show the students how **her** + **e** = **here**. Use a phrase as a mnemonic.	• Introduce the foundation word. • Use word analysis. • Use storytelling. • Develop a mnemonic.
Sample Mnemonic I found **her e here**. [**her** + **e** = **here**] 	**Your Mnemonic**

jump

Foundation words bum

Target word jump

Common error jum, misprinted/reversed letters

Instructional sequence of words

bum   bump jump

New words

dump, hump, lump, pump, rump
mump(s), clump, grump, stump
(enrichment words)

Discussion	Strategies
• Ask the students to spell **bum**. There will be lots of snickering. Next, have them add a letter to spell **bump**.	• Use the foundation word. • Add a letter.
• Ask the students to change **bump** so that it spells **jump**.	• Change a letter.
• Direct the students' attention to the whole word. Tell them that **jump** is in the middle of a big swimming pool. Draw a wavy line on the right and left sides of the word. Focus on the letter **j**. Discuss where a person would stand to jump into the water from the letter **j** (From the tip of the curve in **j** — If you jump from the top of **j**, you will land in the curve of **j**.) Tell the group that a person would always jump from the round top of the **p**.	• Use visual cues, letter configuration.
• Show the students what happens if the letters **j** and **p** are turned the wrong way. If you try to **jump** from the reversed **j**, you will hit your head on the **u**. If you try to **jump** from the round part of the reversed letter **p**, you land on the letter **m**.	
• Develop a mnemonic associated with the visual cues.	• Develop a mnemonic.
Sample Mnemonic Look before you **jump** into the pool.	**Your Mnemonic**

know

Foundation words no

Target word know

Common error no, kno

Instructional sequence of words

no   know

New words

bow, low, mow, row, show, slow
sow, stow, tow

Discussion	Strategies
• Have students print **no** on their slates.	• Use the foundation word.
• Ask them if they **know** a secret (perhaps about a surprise party). Ask the students if you are supposed to tell someone about a surprise party. Ask them why a surprise party should be kept a secret. (Because the party won't be a surprise if you let the person know about it.) Tell them that the word **know** has two secret letters.	• Use word analogy and word analysis.
• Print **no** on the board, and then insert the **k** (the first secret letter), and then the **w**. These are secret letters because we don't say them or hear them.	• Use phonemic awareness.
• Use the idea of a surprise party to make a simple mnemonic.	• Develop a mnemonic.
• Ask students if they notice any symmetry in the word. They may see that the two-letter word is in the middle, and there are two silent letters, one on either end, **k** and **w**.	• Use a mathematical concept.

Sample Mnemonic	Your Mnemonic
I **know** something you don't **know**. Shhhhhh!!! It's a secret!	

little

Foundation words	it, bit, fit, hit, sit, lit
Target word	little
Common error	litl, littel, lidl

Instructional sequence of words

it   lit   little

New words

Discussion	Strategies
• The word **little** is important. Use it to establish the **-le** sequence in words with a final **l** sound. The silent **e** makes **little** tricky.	
• Have the children spell **it**, add a letter, and change a letter to spell the other foundation words.	• Use the foundation words and word analysis.
• Have the group say **little** so that they can hear the last **l** sound and feel the position of the tongue as they say it.	• Use phonemic awareness. • Use kinesthetics to identify the position of the tongue.
• If necessary talk about the meaning of "twins" (two things that are the same).	• Make a mathematical analogy.

• Print **little** on the chalkboard and tell the following story.
 	
   There are six children in the **little** family. The **little** family has two sets of twins. Which letters are the twins? (**l** and **t**) The two letters **l** are the oldest children. We know this because they are the tallest. Who is next oldest in the **little** family? (The two letters **t**, because they are the next tallest.) Who do you think comes next, the **i** or the **e**? (The dotted **i** is taller than the **e**, so **i** is older.)
   When the children in the **little** family go to the park, one of the **l** twins always goes first. This **l** takes care of **i**. The **tt** always stay together. The other **l** comes next, and takes care of baby **e**. The **e** is the youngest and always comes last when we spell **little**.
	• Tell a story.

• Develop a mnemonic based on the story.	• Develop a mnemonic.
Sample Mnemonic There are six children in the **little** family. 	**Your Mnemonic**

look

Foundation words   (not applicable)

Target word   look

Common error   lok

Instructional sequence of words

look

New words

cook, hook, nook, rook, took
brook, crook

Discussion	Strategies
• On the board, focus on the word **look**. Ask for ideas about how to remember the two letters **o** in **look**.	• Use word analogy and word analysis.
• Make a pair of glasses or eyes out of the **-oo-** and ask how this might be useful in remembering how to spell **look**.	• Use a visual, and provide a strong example for visualizing the word.
• Ask the group how they can change **look** into **book**. What other words can they make with **-ook** ending? (e.g., **cook**, **hook**.)	• Use phonemic awareness.

Sample Mnemonic	Your Mnemonic
Use your eyes and **look**.	

new

Foundation words cow, now

Target word   new

Common error   noo

Instructional sequence of words

cow   now   new

New words

dew, few, drew

Discussion	Strategies
• Review the correct spelling of **cow**. Ask the students to change one letter to spell **now**.	• Use foundation words. • Use word analysis; change a letter.
• Print the letters **e** and **o** on the chalkboard, and discuss their shapes. Point out that **e** has a similar shape to **o**.	• Use visual cues and letter configuration.
• Show the students how to modify an **o** into an **e**. Ask the students to print the word **now** on their boards. Tell them to make one change, so **now** is **new**. (Demonstrate this on the classroom chalkboard if necessary.)	• Apply problem solving skills.
• Develop a mnemonic based on changing one letter so that **now** is **new**.	• Use a mnemonic.

Sample Mnemonic	Your Mnemonic
Make one change so **now** is **new**.	

once

Foundation words **one**

Target word **once**

Common error **onse, onec, wuns, wunc, onc**

Instructional sequence of words   New words

on   one   once

Discussion	Strategies
• Review how to spell **one**.	• Use the foundation word.
• Introduce the word **once**, and talk about the meaning of **once**: **one** time.	• Provide a meaning.
• Ask what *sounds* students *hear* in the word **once** (w u n s). Point out that the sounds do not match the letters.	
• Discuss the kind of stories that begin with **once**. (Fairy tales: **Once** upon a time…) Ask for the names of some fairy tales. If you do not elicit *Cinderella*, suggest it.	• Use the word in context.
• Have students visualize a book or video of Cinderella. What is the first letter they see in their minds? The letter **C** in Cinderella has the same sound as the letter **c** in **once**.	• Use visualization. • Use phonemic awareness with visual clues.
• When you print **once** on the board, show the students that Cinderella's two stepsisters are sitting on the left, and her stepmother is on the right.	
• Develop a mnemonic to help students remember that the **s**-sound in **once** is made by the letter **c**.	• Develop a mnemonic.

Sample Mnemonic	Your Mnemonic
Once upon a time... **Once** upon a time, Cinderella lived with her two stepsisters and her stepmother.	

one

Foundation words **on**

Target word **one**

Common error **wun, won**

Instructional sequence of words

on   one

New words

someone, none ("not one")

Discussion	Strategies
• Invite students to print **on**.	• Use the foundation word.
• Print **on** on the chalkboard. Add the letter **e**, and as you do so, tell the group, "You need to "add **on**" **one** letter to make **on** spell **one**." Three letters make **one**. Show them: **on + [1 letter] e = one**	• Use word analysis; add a letter. • Use a reference to mathematics: three letters make one.
• Talk about the tricky part of **one**: it isn't spelled the way it sounds. It sounds as though it should be spelled **wun**.	• Use phonemic awareness.
• Help the students create a mnemonic to remind them that **on** + **e** makes **one**, that suggests they think about where they start a board game.	• Use a mnemonic.
Sample Mnemonic We start **on one** when we play a board game.	**Your Mnemonic**

our, out

Foundation words (not applicable)

Target word **our, out**

Common errors **ar, owr, owt**

Instructional sequence of words

ou   ouch

     our

     out

New words

sour
hour (enrichment)
about, bout, pout, shout

Discussion	Strategies
• Explain that there are two ways of making the **ow** sound. At the beginning or middle of words, the **ow** sound is usually made with **ou**. When it is at the end of a word, it is usually spelled with an **ow** as in **cow**.	• Use a "spelling probability."
• Print **cow** and **ouch** on the board. Read them aloud with the students.	
• Have the students print **ouch** on their boards. Ask the students to change the **ch** to **r**. Ask, "What word does that make?" (**our**) Next, ask them how they could change **our** to spell **out** (change the **r** to **t**)	• Use phonemic awareness. • Use word analysis; change a letter.

• Tell a story that uses the words **ouch**, **our**, and **out**.
 	
    Two mice were in their yard enjoying the sunshine. A big elephant came along. The elephant was actually afraid of mice, but he didn't want them to know. Instead, he was mean. He stepped on their tails.
    "**Ouch**!" yelled the mice. "Oh, you [u] big bully! Get off **our** tails and **out** of our yard!"
	• Use visual cues and a visual aid.

• Review **ou** + **r** and **ou** + **t**. Develop a mnemonic to help students remember the **ou-** sequence in **our** and **out**.	• Develop a mnemonic.
Sample Mnemonic **Ou**ch! **O**h, you [**u**] big bully! Get **out** of **our** yard! Ouch! [ou] Oh [o] you [u] big bully! Get **out** of **our** yard!	**Your Mnemonic**

73

Foundation words (not applicable)

Target word   pull

Common errors   pol, pul

Instructional sequence of words

pull

New words

bull, full

pull

Discussion	Strategies

• Give the word "**pull**" a context by using it in a story.
 	
  A boy and a girl were walking together. They were talking about their pets. They didn't notice the deep hole until they fell into it!
    "Help! Help!" they cried.
    Finally, firefighters arrived to rescue them. One firefighter threw one rope down into the hole. Another firefighter rushed over with another rope and said, "We need two ropes because we have to **pull** up two people!"
	• Tell a story.

• Invite the students to print **pull**. Ask them, "What two letters in **pull** are like ropes?" (**ll**) Tell students to look closely at the first two letters of **pull**. What small word can be made from **p** and **u**? (**up**) Develop a mnemonic.	• Develop a mnemonic.
• Provide the Activity Sheet template and ask students to carefully print **pull** at the top of the page. Then give them time to draw and color a picture that illustrates the mnemonic.	• Use an art activity to associate and reinforce visual cues with the mnemonic.

Sample Mnemonic	Your Mnemonic
We need two ropes to **pull** them up.	

said

Foundation words day, say

Target word said

Common errors sed

Instructional sequence of words

day   say   [sayd]   said

New words

Discussion	Strategies
• Review the spelling of **day**. Ask students to change one letter to spell **say**.	• Use the foundation words.
• Discuss several examples of words that end in **y**. Then explain that when there is a **y** at the end of a word, the **y** is usually changed to an **i** when you add letters to the word. Teach this concept as a "probability rule." Some students may find it helpful to remember that "**y** rhymes with **i**." (Examples could include: fry, fries; bunny, bunnies; try, tried.)	• Use a "probability idea"; use a mnemonic to remember the "spelling probability" (**y** rhymes with **i**).
• Have the students print **say** on their boards. Ask them, "What is the last sound you hear in the word **said**? Print the letter for that sound at the end of **say**." (**say** + **d** = **sayd**) When students have printed **sayd**, ask them what should happen to the **y**. Let the students make the change, and ask someone to spell **said** out loud so that you can print it on the chalkboard.	• Use phonemic awareness; apply the "spelling probability."
• Repeat the probability idea and use **say** and **said** in context in a sentence. Use the sentence as a mnemonic.	• Use the word in context and develop a mnemonic.
Sample Mnemonic **I said**, "What did you **say**?" (The "**I**" can remind students that there is an **i** in **said**.) A a B b C c D d E e F f G g H h I i J j K k L l M m N n s a y + d. (The y probably changes to an i.) s a i d. I said, "What did you say?	**Your Mnemonic**

saw

Foundation words (not applicable)

Target word **saw**

Common errors **sow**

Instructional sequence of words

saw

New words

law, paw, raw
[claw, flaw, slaw, craw, draw
straw (all enrichment)]

Discussion	Strategies
• Print **saw** on the chalkboard. Read it aloud with the group. Discuss the meanings for **saw** (past tense of see, and a tool for cutting wood).	• Model the correct spelling for students.
• Point out the **w**. Draw a **saw** on the board. Ask the students what letter the saw's teeth look like.	• Provide a context for the word.
• Show how the letter **a** looks like a log with a saw cutting the edge.	• Use visual cues and visualization of the shape of the word or letters.
• Develop a mnemonic that helps students recall the image of the saw.	• Develop a mnemonic.
Sample Mnemonic I **saw** grandpa cut the log with his **saw**.	**Your Mnemonic**

seven, eleven

Foundation words eve, even

Target words seven, eleven

Common errors sevn, sevin, elvn, elven, elevin

Instructional sequence of words

eve

even seven eleven

New words

seventy (enrichment)
seventeen (enrichment)

Discussion	Strategies
• Review the meaning and spelling of **eve/Eve**.	• Identify the foundation word.
• Ask students to add one letter to make the word **even**. Ask students where they would print the **s** to make the word **seven**.	• Use word analysis; add a letter.
• Discuss the concept of even and odd numbers, using a few examples. Then ask students if they think **seven** is an odd or an even number. Print **seven** on the board, underline e v e n. Animate the **seven**. Tell the students that in mathematics, **seven** *is* an odd number. When we spell **seven**, it wants to fool us and make us think it is an "even" number.	• Use the students' understanding of mathematical concepts.
• Ask students what number rhymes with **seven** (**eleven**). Print **seven** on the board, and ask students how to change it to make the word **eleven**. Discuss even and odd numbers again. Ask if **eleven** is trying to fool us, too.	• Use rhyme and basic numeracy.
• Develop a mnemonic using the concept of even and odd numbers.	• Develop a mnemonic.

Sample Mnemonic	Your Mnemonic
Seven and **eleven** are not "**even**" numbers. *Yes they are!*	

soon

Foundation words **moo, moon**

Target word **soon**

Common errors **son**

Instructional sequence of words

moo

moon soon

New words

baboon, balloon, cartoon, goon loon, noon, spoon

Discussion	Strategies
• Talk about the rhyming phrases, "See you later, alligator" and "In a while, crocodile."	• Use rhyming phrases.
• Invite students to imagine two cows in a field, saying good-bye to each other. Have the students spell the noise a cow makes (**moo**).	• Identify the foundation word.
• Have students add one letter to make the word **moon**, then change one letter to make the word **soon**.	• Use word analysis; add a letter; change a letter. • Use phonemic awareness.
• Show some pictures of different animals, including a baboon. Name the animals as you show the pictures. Which animal rhymes with **soon**? (**baboon**) Print both words on the board after students have tried to spell them.	• Use visuals.
• Develop a rhyming phrase using **soon** and **baboon** as a mnemonic. As an activity, the children could use the template line master to illustrate two cows saying good bye. One cow should use the mnemonic the group develops for **soon**. Students can print this as a word balloon in their illustration.	• Develop a mnemonic.
Sample Mnemonic See you **soon**, you big **baboon**.	**Your Mnemonic**

there

Foundation words **the, here**

Target word **there**

Common errors **thar**

Instructional sequence of words

the   here   there

New words

Discussion	Strategies
• Review the spelling of **here**.	• Use the foundation words.
• Develop a mnemonic using the following riddle: Where are the only two places in the world you can be that are found in one word? [**here** and **there**; **there**]	• Problem solving.
• Ask students how these two words are combined to spell **there**.	• Use visuals of the two foundation words and how they overlap.
• Write the word **here**. Add one letter to make the word **there**.	• Develop a mnemonic.

Sample Mnemonic

When I am **here**, you are **there**.

I am here and you are there.

No, I am here, you are there.

AaBbCcDdEeFfGgHhIiJjKkLlMmNn

the   here

there

Your Mnemonic

they

Foundation words **the, he, [hey]**

Target words **they**

Common errors **tha, thay**

Instructional sequence of words

they

New words

Discussion	Strategies
• Print **they** on the chalkboard, and invite the students to find the tricky part of the word. Some students might suggest the silent **y**, but most will agree that the trickiest part is the sound made by the **e**. It does not make an **e**-sound. Instead, it says **a**'s name.	• Use word analysis.
• Ask the students to find smaller words in **they** (**the**, **he**). (Really fluent readers and spellers might suggest **hey**.) Erase **they** from the chalkboard.	• Chunk the word into smaller words.
• Ask students if they have heard of the YMCA. Talk briefly about the recreational facilities there. Tell the students that many people call the YMCA *the* **Y** for short. Print *the* **Y** on the board. Ask the students what word has the same letters (**they**).	• Provide a context. Use a word analogy.
• If there is no YMCA in the local area, you might use the idea of a "**Y**" in the road.	
• With the students, develop a mnemonic for **they** based on the words **the Y** and **they**.	• Develop a mnemonic.
Sample Mnemonic **They** met them at **the Y**. They *met at the Y.*	**Your Mnemonic**

three

Foundation words see, tree

Target word three

Common errors thre, thee, tree

Instructional sequence of words

see   tree   three

New words
fee, tee
flee, glee, free
agree (enrichment)

Discussion	Strategies
• Review the pronunciation of the **th** in **three**. Discuss the position of the tongue when we say **th**. (The tongue is caught between the upper and lower front teeth.)	• Use phonemic awareness and kinesthetics (Identify the physical position of the tongue in pronunciation.)
• Invite the students to spell **see**. Talk about the double **ee**. Ask the students for other words that end with double **ee**. (Tree is likely to be suggested. If not, suggest it yourself.)	• Use a foundation word and word analysis. • Use word patterns and word families; rhyming words.
• Print **tree** and **three** on the board. Say **tree**, then say **three**. Ask the students to name the letter that changes **tree** to **three** (the **h**).	• Use word analysis; add a letter.
• Refer to **three** on the board. Ask how many letters come after the **th** in **three** (there are three). Point out that the word **three** represents the number 3.	• Refer to mathematical knowledge.
• Use a visual that has **th** on the left, and three objects that are the same. In the correct order, each of the objects contains the letters **r e e**. Create a mnemonic.	• Develop a mnemonic.
Sample Mnemonic I **see** there are [r] **three**. I **see** there are [r] three.	**Your Mnemonic**

two

Foundation words   (not applicable)

Target word   two

Common errors   to, too, tow, tu

Instructional sequence of words   New words

two

Discussion	Strategies

• The word **two** lends itself to visualization. Tell students a story that can be used as a mnemonic that will help them visualize the whole word.
 	
   Ask students to imagine a tall person. (Print **t** on the board.) The tall person was very hungry one day, and decided to have **two** ice cream cones.
   (Print **w** beside the **t**.) Ask the students if they can see the **two** ice cream cones. (Draw ice cream cones in the **w**.)
   As the tall person left the store with **two** ice cream cones, the scoop of ice cream fell off one of them. "Oh, no! Now I will still be hungry!" said the tall person. (Print the letter **o** after the **w**, to make **two**.)
   As an alternative, students could think of the letter **o** as the scoop of ice cream that falls off one of the cones.
 	
• For the mnemonic device, students should recall the tall person (**t**), the **two** ice cream cones (**w**), and the "Oh, no!" (**o**) when the ice cream falls off one of the cones.
	• Develop a story to help students visualize the shape and letters in the word.
	
	• Create a mnemonic that is associated with visualization of the word and letters.
	
	• Tell a story that matches the visualization.

Sample Mnemonic A **t**all person had **two** ice cream cones. 	**Your Mnemonic**

walk

Foundation words (not applicable)

Target word **walk**

Common errors **wok**

Instructional sequence of words

walk

New words

talk, chalk
stalk (enrichment)

Discussion	Strategies
• Ask the students if they have any pets. Talk briefly about cats, birds, etc., then focus on dogs and things that dogs like to do. Students will likely say that dogs like to play Frisbee, ball, and go for a walk. Students will agree that most dogs like to go for **a long walk**.	• Establish a context for learning the word.
• Spell **walk** and have students print it. Discuss the tricky parts of the word: It sounds as if it has an **o**, and the **l** is silent.	• Identify the hard parts of the word.
• As students look at the word, ask if they can see any clues about what kind of walk a dog would like. Students could associate the -**al**- with *a **l**ong w**al**k*. Develop a mnemonic based on this idea.	• Use a mnemonic.
Sample Mnemonic My dog likes to go for **a** long **walk**.	**Your Mnemonic**

want

Foundation words ant

Target word want

Common errors wont

Instructional sequence of words   New words

ant   want

Discussion	Strategies
• Talk about occasions when people give or receive gifts. Ask how they decide what to give as a gift. Try to elicit that you think about something the person would like. Some people even ask, "What do you want for your birthday?" Ask the group to suggest some things they might want as gifts.	• Establish a context.
• Remind the students of Yip, the anteater from the lesson for **any**. Ask the group, "What do you think Yip would **want** for his birthday?" (Give them the hint: You can find the answer in the word **want**.)	• Apply problem solving skills.
• Have the students print **want** on their boards. Check their spelling and then print **want** on the classroom chalkboard. If necessary, have students correct their own spelling of **want**.	• Use word analysis.
• Invite them to underline the part of want that answers the question, "What would an anteater **want** for its birthday?" (**want**).	• Model the word for students. • Use the foundation word.
• Use the context to develop a mnemonic with the students.	• Develop a mnemonic.

Sample Mnemonic	Your Mnemonic
What would an anteater **want** for its birthday?	

were

Foundation words we, are

Target word were

Common errors war, where, where

Instructional sequence of words   New words

we   were

Discussion	Strategies
• Ask students to spell **we**. Review how to spell **are**.	• Introduce the foundation words.
• Print the following two sentences on the board and ask students to compare **we are** and **we were**. Today we are going to the store. Yesterday we were going to the store.	• Provide grammatical context.
• Ask for suggestions on how they could remember how to spell **were**. Some students may notice that if you drop the **a** from **we are**, it makes **we re—>were**. Other students may say that you just add **re** to **we**: **we + re = were**.	• Use word analysis; break up the word(s) and add or drop letters to make the correct spelling.
• Develop a mnemonic with the students. Use either of the strategies above, or simply develop a mnemonic that emphasizes **we** in **were**. In addition, you could dictate at random **were** or **where**, and provide them in an appropriate contextual sentence. This allows students to focus on the context in which each word is used. The students should listen for the sound difference as well as the context.	• Develop a mnemonic that uses the word analysis. • Use context and phonemic awareness.

Sample Mnemonic	Your Mnemonic
We were going to the store. AaBbCcDdEeFfGgHhIiJjKkLlMmNn we are we re were	

85

what

Foundation words **at, hat**

Target word **what**

Common errors **wut, wot**

Instructional sequence of words

hat   what

New words

whatever

Discussion	Strategies
• Print **what** on the chalkboard.	
• Ask if the students can see any smaller words in **what**. (**at**, **hat**)	• Introduce the foundation words.
• Have all the students print **what** on their own boards. Show some pictures of different, fancy hats, then ask the students to look at the word **what** on their boards. Go around the group and ask them, "**W**here is your **hat**?" They will likely ask you, "**What hat**?" Point to their board. When they find the **hat** in **what**, have them underline it: <u>what</u>.	• Use a game that involves word analysis.
• Discuss when and why we need to wear a **hat**. Describe a cold winter day. Ask what a teacher might say when the class is dressing for outdoor recess on a cold winter day. Try to elicit, "**W**ear your **hat**!" Use this question as the mnemonic or develop a new one with the group.	• Develop a mnemonic that uses the word analysis.
• In art, students can draw a picture of someone wearing a funny hat to keep warm in the winter.	• Use an art activity to reinforce the concept in the mnemonic.
Sample Mnemonic **W**ear your **hat**! **What** hat?	**Your Mnemonic**

when

Foundation words he, hen

Target word when

Common errors wen

Instructional sequence of words

New words

| he | hen | |
| we | w + hen | when |

Discussion	Strategies
• Print **when** on the chalkboard and read it out loud.	• Model the new word on the board.
• Ask students what words they can see in **when** (**he**, **hen**). Then erase the word **when**.	• Use word analysis; chunk the word (into the foundation words).
• Focus on the words **he**, **hen**. Ask students to print **he** on their boards, and then add a letter to make it spell **hen** (**he** + **n**). Print **hen** on the board.	• Add a letter to spell the new word.
• Ask the students what letter they need to add to **hen** to make **when**. (**w** + **hen** = **when**)	
• Use the image of the hen in a story. One idea is to associate the hen and her eggs with breakfast. (If it is necessary, point out that eggs are an ingredient in many breakfast foods.) Perhaps someone is anxious to have breakfast. "**When** can we have breakfast?" The answer could be, "**When** the **hen** lays an egg."	• Use a mnemonic that identifies the tricky letters.
• Develop a mnemonic.	• Use a mnemonic that creates a vivid visual cue in the students' minds.
Sample Mnemonic **When** can we have breakfast? **When** the **hen** lays an egg.	**Your Mnemonic**

Be patient! When the hen lays an egg, we'll have breakfast.

where

Foundation word   here
Target words   where
Common errors   wer wher were

Instructional sequence of words   New words

here   where

Discussion	Strategies
• Have students print **here** on their boards. Ask them to add one letter to spell **where**.	• Use the foundation word and word analysis.
• While the students are printing on their boards, ask them **where** something is (e.g., "**Where** is your pen?") The students answer this question by underlining **here** in w<u>here</u>.	• Use the word in context.
• Print "We are here." on the classroom board. Then ask the students, "Where are we?" You will probably get a chorus of "We are here!" Ask them again as you erase the letters **e a r e** (one at a time), thus making the remaining letters spell **where**. Let the students go through the procedure on their own boards.	• Use word analysis; erase letters to make the correct word.
• Develop a mnemonic and print it on the board.	• Use a mnemonic that creates a vivid visual cue in the students' minds.

Sample Mnemonic	Your Mnemonic
"**Where** are **we**?" "**We** are **here**."	

88

which

Foundation words (not applicable)

Target word which

Common errors wich

Instructional sequence of words New words

which

Discussion	Strategies
• Talk about twins. Find out how much students know about twins. Do they know any twins? Can they tell one twin from the other?	• Establish a context for learning the word.
• Print the word **which**. Do the students see any letters that would be twins? (**h** and **h**).	
• Ask students how they might use **w** + **h** and **c** + **h** to tell one twin from the other twin. The twin with **wh** has **w**avy **h**air and the twin with **ch** has **c**urly **h**air.	• Develop a mnemonic.
• **Which** twin is **which**? The twin with **wh** has **w**avy **h**air and the twin with **ch** has **c**urly **h**air. Have the students draw the twins. They can print **wh** and **ch** under the appropriate twin.	• Use an art activity to reinforce the letters visually.
Sample Mnemonic	**Your Mnemonic**
Which twin is **which**? The twin with **wh** has **w**avy **h**air and the twin with **ch** has **c**urly **h**air.	

Foundation words **we, hit**

Target word **white**

Common errors **wite**

Instructional sequence of words

we   hit   white

white

New words

Discussion	Strategies
• Using **it**, **hit**, **we**, and **white**, tell a story about playing baseball. In the summer, **we** played baseball with all the children in the park. Some of us were good at throwing and catching the ball. **We** all had a chance to **hit it**. **We hit** the ball so hard **it** broke the window of a **white** house. The owner came out and asked, "Who **hit** that ball and broke my window?" No one said a word. • Tell the students there are clues in the word **white** that would help the owner find out who broke the window. Have the students print **we** and **hit** on their boards. Check their spellings, then put the words on the classroom chalkboard, with **we** above **hit**. Talk about the word **white**. What sound does it start with? (**w**) Is the **i** in **white** a long or a short vowel sound? (**long**) Now, ask the students to look at the words **we** and **hit**. Tell the students to take a letter from **we** that can be added to **hit** to make the **i** say its name (**hit + e**). Ask them where they would put the **w** to make the word **white**. (**w + hite**) • Print the word **white** on the board. Ask students to associate the words **we**, **hit**, and **white** to develop a mnemonic.	• Use storytelling. • Apply phonemic awareness. • Use the foundation words. • Word analysis; break the word into smaller words; add a letter. • Develop a mnemonic.
Sample Mnemonic Who **hit** the **white** ball? **We hit** the **white** ball. (Students can underline the letters that make the word **we**, and use a different colour to print the letters **hit**.) **w h i t e**	**Your Mnemonic**

90

who

Foundation words   (not applicable)

Target word   who

Common errors   how, hu

Instructional sequence of words

who

New words

Discussion	Strategies

• Use the word who in several contextual questions.
  • **Who** has freckles?
  • **Who** has a pet?
  • **Who** has eyes?
	• Develop a context; use the word.

• Explain what an acronym is. Then invite the students to make acronyms for the **who** questions you asked (e.g., **Who** has freckles? (**WHF**) If the answer is "Tina has freckles," the acronym for that would be, **THF**.	• Phonemic awareness; discuss the tricky parts of the word.
• After using **who** in several contextual sentences, let students suggest some **who** sentences.	• Model the word.
• Repeat the spelling of **who**. Have students print **who** on their boards.	
• Use the letters **w**, **h**, and **o** as the first letter of words (in the correct sequence) in an acronym to help them remember the correct spelling.	• Develop an acronym as a mnemonic.

Sample Mnemonic	Your Mnemonic
Who **h**as **o**ranges? **W**e **h**ave **o**ranges. W ho W e h as h ave **o**ranges? **o**ranges!	

Foundation words   (not applicable)

Target words   **would, should, could**

Common errors   **wud, wood, shud, shood, cud, cold**

Instructional sequence of words   New words

would
should
could

would, should, could

Discussion	Strategies
• Print **would**, **should**, and **could** on the chalkboard. Talk about the letters that these three words have in common. You might want to suggest that the words are "cousins" because they have the same four last letters. Next, ask students to identify the sounds in each word and the letters that make them. Students will quickly see that **ou** is not making its usual sound, and the **l** is silent. These four letters **o u l d** are the tricky part of these words.	• Phonemic awareness; word analysis.
• Talk about acronyms with students, (e.g., CBC: Canadian Broadcasting Corporation; NASA: National Air and Space Association). When students are familiar with the concept of acronyms, ask them to help you develop an acronym for the tricky letters in **would**, **should**, and **could** (e.g., **O**h, yo**u l**azy **d**og! **Would** you like to go for a walk ? I **should** take you for a walk, so you **could** play ball with me.).	• Use an acronym as a mnemonic.
Sample Mnemonic Use the acronym as the mnemonic: **O**h, yo**u l**azy **d**og! I **would** like to take you for a walk! I **could** take you for a walk! I **should** take you for a walk! *Oh, you lazy dog!* *I **would** like to take you for a walk!* *I **could** take you for a walk!* *I **should** take you for a walk!*	**Your Mnemonic**

Foundation words (letters) I O U

Target words *you*

Common errors *yoo, yu*

Instructional sequence of words

you   our   your

New words

you

Discussion	Strategies
• Print **I.O.U.** on the board. Ask if anyone can explain what it means. Students can role play lending money and signing an **I.O.U.**	• Provide a context.
• Talk about the letter **i**. Remind the students that **y** sometimes takes the place of **i**. Ask for or provide some examples such as **tries**, **try**; **crystal**.	• Use phonemic awareness and a "spelling probability."
• Ask the students to print **i.o.u.** on their boards. Have them change the **i** to **y**. Introduce a mnemonic phrase to help students associate **you** with **i.o.u.**	• Develop a vivid visual image and an accompanying mnemonic.

Sample Mnemonic	**Your Mnemonic**
I owe you some money.  	

Foundation words *you, our*

Target words *your*

Common errors *yor*

Instructional sequence of words

you   our   your

New words

Discussion	Strategies
• Review the spelling of **you** and **our**. Use **you** as the foundation word (**you + r**), or **our** as the foundation word (**y + our**). Some students do not recognize the phonemic or grammatical connection between **you** and **your** because of the slight change in the pronunciation of the vowels. Similarly, **our** and **your** do not sound alike, but the two words share the same grammatical function in a sentence.	• Use the foundation words. • Use word analysis.
• Discuss the meaning of **your**: It indicates that **you** own something (e.g., *You* may bring **your** pig.) Use other possessive forms (*I* - **my**, *he* - **his**, *she* - **hers**, *they* - **their**) as reinforcement for the concept. (It is usually best to use the same example for each possessive pronoun.)	• Develop the grammatical context.
• Develop a mnemonic that uses the words in the correct grammatical context.	• Use a mnemonic that creates a vivid visual cue in the students' minds.

Sample Mnemonic	Your Mnemonic
Our home is **your** home, so you may bring **your** pig!	

Our home is your home, so you may bring your pig!

3 Student Activity Sheets

A Word About the Student Activity Sheets

These student activity sheets are provided as a follow-up to the lesson and discussion for eleven specific high frequency words in this book. Each student activity includes blank lines where students are to print how they remember how to spell each word.

A blank activity sheet template that can be used for any spelling word is provided on the next page so that you can develop your own follow-up activities. The drawings that students do on the student activity sheets serve as a visual for the context or meaning of the mnemonic, which comes out of the discussion or storytelling in the lesson. Initially, you may have to provide the ideas for pictures (or the actual pictures) for the words, but students will soon become more independent at creating their own.

These student activity sheets are for reinforcement and should be distributed one at a time to weaker students or to students who are having difficulty with a particular word or concept.

Students enjoy and can benefit from keeping their completed activity sheets in a booklet, which they can use as a beginning dictionary of learned words. During writing activities, students can refer to their dictionaries. These booklets can also serve as a portfolio to share with parents, so they can see the words and lessons their child is doing in spelling.

Name: _____   Spelling Word:_____

What to Do

_____
_____
_____
_____

_____

_____

big

Name: _____

Here is a picture of someone fishing.

What does she need to catch a fish? Draw a circle around the bait, the line and the sinker, and the hook. Draw a picture of the fish she wants to catch. Now color the whole picture.

Print the word **big** on this line. _____

How do you remember how to spell **big**? Print your answer here.

_____

_____

Name: _____

eight

Look at the ribbon in the picture. Trace over the letters. They are the first 8 letters of the alphabet.

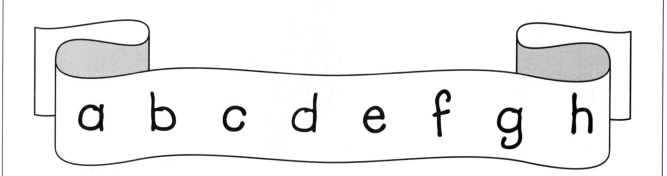

Where would you cut the ribbon to cut off the first 4 letters?

Draw a line there.

Now draw a picture of what you would do with this piece of ribbon.

Print the word **eight** on this line. _____

How do you remember how to spell **eight**? Print your answer here.

_____

_____

Name: _____

This is a treasure chest that you found in a cave. Fill the treasure chest with things you would like to find in it.

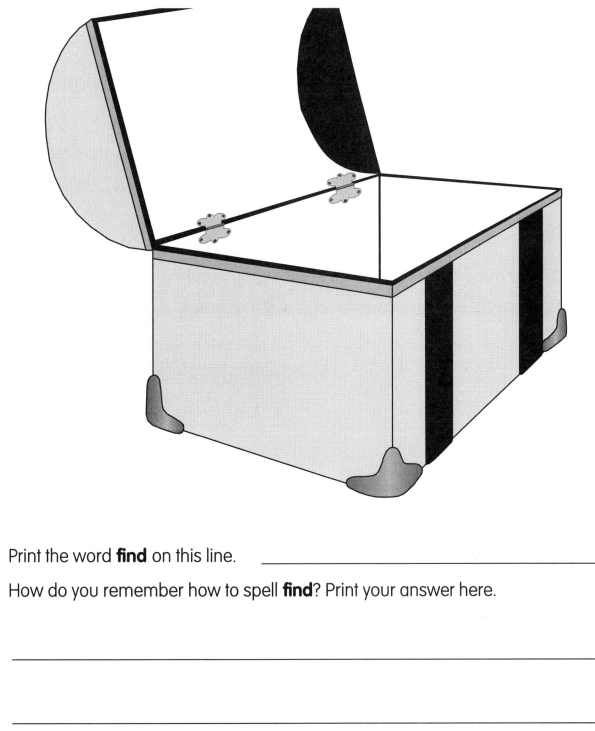

Print the word **find** on this line. _____

How do you remember how to spell **find**? Print your answer here.

_____

_____

Name: _____

This postcard is from Tom. Print your name and address on the lines on the postcard.

To my friend,	ADDRESS:
It is fun here. We have done lots of new things. We are leaving for home tomorrow. I will see you soon.	_____
	_____
	_____
From Tom	_____

The postcard needs a stamp. Draw a pretty stamp in the box below.

Print the word **from** on this line. _____

How do you remember how to spell **from**? Print your answer here.

_____

_____

funny

Name: _____

Here is a picture of the children in the funny family. Color the picture. Do not forget about the triplets. They should be in the same clothes.

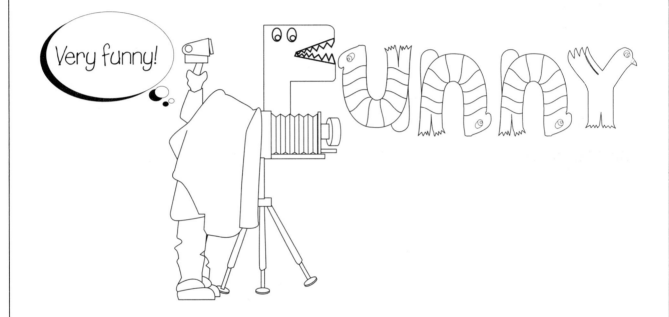

Print the word **funny** on this line. _____

How do you remember how to spell **funny**? Print your answer here.

_____

_____

help

Name: _____

The boy in this picture is in trouble. He has fallen down a steep cliff. Draw a man with a rope trying to help the boy.

Print the word **help** on this line. _____

How do you remember how to spell **help**? Print your answer here.

_____

_____

little

Name: _____

Here is the little family. They are going to see something exciting. Where do you think they are going?

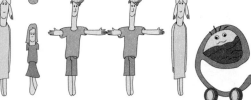

Draw a picture that shows what they will see. Use lots of color and details.

Print the word **little** on this line. _____

How do you remember how to spell **little**? Print your answer here.

_____

_____

Name: _____

These people are going to play a game. Draw a circle around the number where they should start. Now, color the picture.

Print the word **one** on this line. _____

How do you remember how to spell **one**? Print your answer here.

_____

_____

two

Name: _____

Look at this picture. What letter looks like two ice cream cones?

Color the picture and make the scoops of ice cream look like your two favorite flavors. When you are done, ask a friend to guess what your favorite flavors are.

Print the word **two** on this line. _____

How do you remember how to spell **two**? Print your answer here.

_____

_____

Name: _____

This is Binky the dog. Binky went for a long walk with a boy and a girl. He is not tired, but the boy and girl are! Draw the boy and girl. Make them look tired. How will their faces look? What about their hair and clothes?

Print the word **walk** on this line. _____

How do you remember how to spell **walk**? Print your answer here.

_____

_____

Name: _____

This student is going outside for recess. The teacher says, "Wear your hat!" What do you think the student says to the teacher? Print the answer on the lines in the word balloon. Then, draw a funny hat so the student isn't cold outside. Color the whole picture.

Print the word **what** on this line. _____

How do you remember how to spell **what**? Print your answer here.

_____

_____

4 Teacher Evaluation Tools

A Word About Teacher Evaluation Tools

Lesson Observation Notes is a helpful tool for recording specific target words and their foundation words, as well as points elicited from the group discussion and the student's mnemonic.

Student Test Records offers a chart for recording test scores for the classroom teacher's own spelling lists. There are spaces for up to four tests per list because some students may need to be tested several times before they achieve mastery of the list.

Progress Reports helps teachers track each individual student's work in spelling. Teachers can use checkmarks to note if a word is new or if the student is in a learning phase for the word. The difficulties the student is encountering can also be recorded. The last column is checked off when the student has achieved mastery of the target word. At a glance, teachers (and parents) can see the progress of and challenges for the student.

Lesson Observation Notes

Target Word	Foundation Words	Common Errors	Discussion Notes	Student's Mnemonic(s)
again	rain	agen, agian	Need to reinforce "ai" to make "a" say its name	Will it rain again?

Student Test Records

Student Name	Spelling List # ___				Spelling List # ___				Spelling List # ___			
	Score for Test # __	Score for Test # __	Score for Test # __	Score for Test # __	Score for Test # __	Score for Test # __	Score for Test # __	Score for Test # __	Score for Test # __	Score for Test # __	Score for Test # __	Score for Test # __

Progress Reports

Student: _____

Target Word	Student's Progress			
	New Word	Learning	Difficulties	Mastered
again	✓		"ia" instead of "ai"	